My Spirit Rejoices

MY SPIRIT REJOICES

Imagining and Praying the Magnificat with Mary

MARCI ALBORGHETTI

TWENTY
THIRD 23rd
PUBLICATIONS
www.23rdpublications.com

TWENTY-THIRD PUBLICATIONS

1 Montauk Avenue, Suite 200, New London, CT 06320

(860) 437-3012 » (800) 321-0411 » www.23rdpublications.com

ISBN: 978-1-62785-045-2

Library of Congress Catalog Card Number: 2015947544

Printed in the U.S.A.

FOR GOD,
AND THE
MOTHER OF
HIS CHILD.

TO CHARLIE.

CONTENTS

INTRODUCTION

WHAT IS YOUR IMAGE OF MARY?

Do you see her as "Our Blessed Mother," a gently smiling matriarch looking down upon us benevolently, always there to help and understand? Is your vision that of a calm, collected, proud young mother holding the newborn Jesus out for shepherds and wise men alike to admire? Do you see her as the grieving mother of the Pietà, holding her Son's broken body in her arms, displaying a grief so agonizingly contained it can only be imagined? Do you see her as a travel companion to Jesus and the apostles, kind of like an efficient, uncomplaining den mother, there to manage all the details of their travel arrangements? Or is she the stern, straight-backed woman who is crushing a serpent under her foot while holding a lily, or even the infant Jesus, in her arms? Do you perceive her mainly as an intercessor, the one you turn to when you're afraid to turn to God and need her help explaining your latest request or transgression? Do you imagine her as the Queen of Heaven, wearing a lovely, flowing robe and jewel-encrusted crown while looking down serenely upon us all from on high?

These are all very clear—and very real—visions of Mary for most of us. They may even be accurate. We have seen these images in Bible illustrations, movies, paintings, and statues in our churches and homes. They are pious, appropriate, and safe images. They are explicable and comprehensible—and very, very constrained.

They also do not do Mary credit. They allow us to make her into what we want, what we *need*, her to be. They limit and inevitably diminish her, locating her squarely on the narrow road that we need her to travel.

When I was young, though probably not much younger than Mary at the time Gabriel visited her, I was fascinated by a children's Bible illustration of Mary that has stuck in my mind ever since. She is in a very simple room, presumably the home she shared with her parents, and she is...dusting! Yes, she has a rag in her hand and she is dusting a crude chair set near a crude table. And she is smiling. She is just a girl doing her chores, and I can remember being amazed, not so much at the idea of Mary as a girl doing chores— since I had not yet had so many other, more typical, images imprinted on my brain—but because one of *my* household chores was to dust the dining room table and chairs.

Mary had to do what I had to do every single day! Not that I did it with a smile, which may say more about me than about Mary, but nevertheless, at that moment she became real to me. Later in the story, of course, Gabriel visited her... perhaps in that very same room while she still held the dust rag. But by then, everything that would happen to Mary going forward carried the background image for me of a girl doing her chores. In other words, I have never been able to forget that she had a life before she became *MARY!*

Mary was a person, perhaps with hopes and dreams that we will never know about. She was a child, however difficult the life of a child in hard-scrabble Nazareth might have been; nonetheless, she was a girl who lived and ate and made friends and played and learned and helped her parents. And dusted.

Then, suddenly, without any warning, she was so much more. When Mary acquiesced to God's plan, she became someone else we—because we have sort of co-opted her as our very own—don't often think about or imagine: a historical figure who quite literally changed the course of humankind. Prophets had described her; complex biblical figures like Sarah, Hannah, and Ruth had prefigured her; and God had prepared for her.

So, she is not just "ours." And she was certainly no longer just "hers" after Gabriel's visit. Still, she was a person in her own right, a person of her own time, a person carrying a blessed burden beyond what most women could even comprehend. Which may well be why we imagine her so narrowly. How can we fathom who she was and who she became and how she did it?

Consider this: Mary was betrothed to Joseph at around the age when many of our children are graduating from middle school or entering their freshman year of high school. She was pregnant with Jesus at about the same time we're worrying about whether our kids paid attention during the sex ed section in their health class. She set out, or perhaps fled, on a difficult, multi-day journey to an older relative she seldom saw and perhaps hardly knew, when we have to drive our kids to the mall or soccer practice a few miles away.

This is the girl-woman who speaks only a few times in the gospels: first, to agree to God's plan that she bear his Son; second, in a positively effusive prayer of praise, the canticle we have come to call the *Magnificat*; twelve years later, to reproach the boy, Jesus, for making her and Joseph worry; and nearly twenty years later, to nudge her Son into his first public miracle, the changing of water to wine at a wedding. That's it. We hear no more from Mary. She is there, surely, and we can guess what she may be thinking, but she does not speak to us. And out of this paucity of real information, we have fashioned our images of Mary.

The *Magnificat* gives us Mary on the fault line between what she had been and what she is becoming. It is so much more than a simple prayer of praise. It is the acknowledgment by an immensely important historical figure of what her role is to be; it is Mary's first and only declaration that she now fully comprehends exactly what is happening: namely, that the entire world has waited for this moment and that her people in particular have waited in both hope and agony for the child she—and she alone—has been chosen to bear.

In these pages, we will meet the Mary who, uncharacteristically it would seem, proclaimed this extraordinary canticle. We will come to know her through her words, and we will explore what they meant for her, for her family, for her people, for history, and for us. Each chapter will address one verse of the *Magnificat* and, please God, bring us into a deeper and more profound understanding of the canticle and its speaker.

ONE

And Mary Said

And Mary said, "My soul magnifies the Lord..."

LUKE 1:46

SETTING THE SCENE

The girl stood at the edge of the small clearing. It was a pretty village, set among the hills of Judea; she had forgotten how pretty. Wild flowers, green trees—so different from her home, Nazareth, in the difficult and distant north. In many ways, it was a different country almost. She had been traveling for almost four days now, and the change had been gradual. She was tired, so tired. And afraid. Just a little afraid. Well, maybe more than a little. It had been some time since she'd visited this place, where her aging relative Elizabeth lived with her even older husband, Zechariah. The homes in this village were set out nicely; they looked inviting. It was easier to make a life here, she thought, than at home.

The girl began to walk slowly toward a particular dwelling. She came to the doorway and stood there, hesitating. Then she saw Elizabeth, and a soft sigh of joyful relief passed through her lips. The older woman inside, hand on her back, belly distended with the child she bore despite her advanced years, peered at the girl in the dim light, her eyes straining, first in curiosity, then disbelief, then pleasure. She hurried as best she could, waddling a bit, toward the girl who still stood rooted to the spot, not out of rudeness—never that with this girl—but something else.

Abruptly, Elizabeth stopped, and her hand moved from her back to her belly. Her eyes widened, and the arm she had extended to embrace Mary froze in the air. She gasped, though not in pain, as Mary watched closely, hopefully. If Mary hadn't prevented her, Elizabeth would have fallen to her knees as she cried out in ecstasy, "Blessed are you among women, and blessed is the fruit of your womb. And why has this happened to me, that the mother of my Lord has come to me? For as soon as I heard the sound of your greeting, the child in my womb leaped for joy" (Luke 1:42–44).

FOR MARY AND HER JUDEAN FAMILY

Imagine Mary's relief! Within the space of a few weeks, this girl barely into her teens has been visited by one of the most powerful angels of heaven, learned that she has been chosen to bear God's Son, and probably struggled with euphoria, terror, and wonderment. Gabriel, knowing that though she was without sin, she was not without a human nature, had given her something to hold onto: he told her that her distant relative Elizabeth, known to be well beyond child-bearing years and humiliated because she had not borne Zechariah a son or even a daughter, was pregnant. Wise Gabriel knew enough about human travail to realize he needed to offer a little more: not only had Elizabeth conceived, she was bearing a son, and she was beyond the typical danger period wherein such an old woman in her first pregnancy was likely to lose the child. Elizabeth, Mary was told, was already in her sixth month. That child, also chosen by God, though for a different purpose, was safe in his mother's womb.

Mary probably hadn't immediately been able to take in all that Gabriel had said. The enormity of his revelation about her was too much on its own, and she'd needed more time to absorb the rest of his words. As the immediate anxiety and excitement generated by Gabriel's visit and words eased just a bit, Mary had begun to wonder about so much. What was happening? How would she cope? What about Joseph, her parents, her neighbors? What would people say? What would they do? Would anyone believe her?

She did not doubt the angel's words to her—about her—nor did she regret her own acceptance of God's plan. To do so would have been not only to reject God—unthinkable!—but to betray her people, who had been waiting for centuries for this. Still, she could not quite take it all in, and she found herself focusing on Gabriel's last words about Elizabeth. She came to think that the angel had given her not only an assurance that needed to be experienced but a way to address her immediate situation.

She needed to get out of Nazareth.

She needed time to understand what she was to do. She needed time to understand how she was to protect God's Son from those who would not understand, who would not believe. Gabriel had not given her a lot of practical information. How was she to keep the zealots in Nazareth and

its environs from rejecting her and her family, maybe even
stoning her as the law of Moses would allow? To them, her
conception could well appear as an adulterous or unlawful
pregnancy. How would she be able to convince them that a
poor girl from Nazareth was to be the fulfillment of prophecies that they had heard and awaited for all their lives, as
had their ancestors for generations before? Just as we may
have to stretch to imagine the real Mary, so would they
have found it difficult to imagine the prophetic virgin as
an impoverished peasant with no family or priestly name
from an outback region of Israel.

And what would Joseph do? How would he respond?
We must remember that at this point, Joseph had not had
a dream from God, had not been visited by a messenger
assuring him that Mary was pregnant with God's Son and
that it was to be his, Joseph's, job to be her husband and
protector.

So, when Mary set out on the long, arduous trip from
Nazareth to Judea, she was, from a human perspective,
simply and starkly alone.

It would have taken several days, depending upon how
she traveled, before she finally arrived in Judea, made
her way to Elizabeth's house, and stood at the threshold.
She had had all that time to think and wonder, hope and
pray. Her faith told her that Elizabeth would be pregnant
as Gabriel had revealed, but Mary was still human. We
must never forget that. Maybe she didn't dust her mother's
kitchen table, but she was human. She had chosen to visit
Elizabeth not only to give herself time to absorb her own
situation, but to follow the lead that Gabriel had given her:
"And now, your relative Elizabeth in her old age has also

conceived a son; and this is the sixth month for her who was said to be barren" (Luke 1:36).

Would Elizabeth be pregnant? Visibly, healthily pregnant?

For Mary, at this point, she *had* to be! Gabriel had given her that assurance as something to cling to in the coming days of confusion, excitement, and even fear. If Elizabeth was pregnant, Mary could be assured that, as Gabriel had said, "nothing will be impossible with God" (Luke 1:37).

Mary can see as the older woman comes to her that Elizabeth is indeed pregnant and in the full bloom of health. But God gives them both an additional gift. Not only is Elizabeth pregnant with the child who will herald the coming of Mary's Son; Elizabeth knows! She recognizes that her young relative has not come for a casual visit. Elizabeth, we are told, knows this not on her own, but through the Holy Spirit. After her own child leaps in her womb at the presence of Jesus-in-Mary, Elizabeth was, Luke tells us, "filled with the Holy Spirit and exclaimed with a loud cry" (Luke 1:41–42).

At that moment, filled with relief and joyous conviction, everything comes together for Mary. Everything she has been taught, everything she knows about Scripture and prophecy, everything she has thought and prayed over since Gabriel's visitation—all of it merges into the core certainty that will carry her through the trial and turmoil and joy of the rest of her life. She comprehends the magnitude of what God has done, and she makes it her own.

And Mary said, "My soul magnifies the Lord."

For the World

By the time Gabriel visited Mary, and Mary visited
Elizabeth and Zechariah, Abraham's children were a people steeped in despair. After spending the first part of their
existence struggling against their own conflicts and the
hatred of the desert nations they would displace to inhab-
it the land God promised them, they enjoyed a period of
relative peace and prosperity, at least compared to what
had come before and what would come after. But shortly
after the great king, David, and his wise son, Solomon, had
been, we are told, buried with their ancestors, things started to fall apart for the Hebrew people.

With very few exceptions, the kings that followed were
weak, evil, or both. They moved—or followed—the people
back into the idolatry that characterized the tribes from
which they came. Jealousies and divisions arose, and eventually the people of God split into two nations, often at
odds, though sometimes coming together against common
enemies. The kingdom of Israel formed to the north, Judah
or Judea to the south. Nazareth, considered an outpost of
civilized life, was in what was then known as Israel, while
the kingdom of Judah possessed the considerable cachet
of Jerusalem and the temple, though it was frequently pillaged and even destroyed during those years.

The Jews became a fragmented people, often separated
from their God, and prey to their warlike neighbors who
had never stopped resenting them for taking the Promised
Land. Great prophets like Isaiah and Jeremiah, Elijah and
Elisha, arose to warn the people and to speak of a future
Messiah, but they did not have the power, or in reality, the
mission from God to reunite the people or free them from

occupying armies. These and many other prophets, however, did increasingly confirm the prophecies of David and Moses, not to mention the veiled promises to Abraham of a coming Messiah who would return the people to their former prosperity and closeness to God.

At the time of Mary's visit to Elizabeth, the Jews were at their collective wits' end. With a brief respite under the Maccabees, they had spent centuries being passed around and exploited by just about every powerful king and warrior-general in the region. They now struggled under the sandal-boot of Rome, ostensibly ruled by an appointee of Caesar, Herod, whom they despised as an impostor and a false Jew. Their economic burden was immense. While we may complain about taxes, the Hebrew people were oppressed to the point of ruination, paying obscenely high taxes to fund Herod's hunger for palaces and ostentatious wealth and Rome's need to fund its infrastructure and empire. The Jews knew nothing of real freedom, either from an economic or a self-governing perspective, and it was simply getting worse and worse.

If there was ever a time for the Messiah, should it not be now?

Such thoughts and hopes were so hot in the hearts and minds of Jews in both the north and south that, in fact, many outliers had arisen to claim, if not that they were the Messiah, that they at least were willing to fight for God's Messiah so that when he came, he would find a free nation ready to serve him. The Romans, with Herod's complicity and occasionally active help, had responded to such rebellions by crushing them and publicly crucifying rebel leaders and their followers. Again and again, the

Jews had been disappointed and disillusioned; however, they *knew* that God would not abandon them. When had he lied to them? Never! When had he not fulfilled his end of any covenant?

Never!

It was just a matter of time, and the Jews, from the uneducated shepherd in the field to the cleverest Pharisee, were on the watch. Their history was replete with evidence of the magnitude of God's power, and now, perhaps more than ever, their need for God's intervention was magnified.

And Mary said, "My soul magnifies the Lord."

For Us

How do we experience Mary today? How do we "hear" or listen to her song of praise? More precisely, how do we hope?

Do we have the faith of our religious ancestors, the Jews? Would any of our daughters—any of us—have even a thimbleful of the courage of Mary, Elizabeth, or Zechariah? Do we believe that God is with us? Do we understand, as the Hebrews did at the dawn of Jesus' coming, how deeply we are in need of God, of the Messiah?

But wait! We have him, don't we? Isn't this old news? Charming and moving, certainly, but nonetheless, past history? Even if we rouse ourselves to consider Mary as a girl, a person, an enormously powerful figure of history, even if we study Scripture and fully understand how the entire world awaited the coming of Jesus, even if we become deeply aware of the condition of the Jews and the world at that time—well, that was then and this is now, right? What does it really mean to us?

Everything. ***Everything!***

We are in the same condition as the Jews at that time. We are disappointed, disillusioned, and cynical. Believers, later to be called Christians, have been waiting for Jesus' return, waiting for the Messiah, almost from the moment of the Ascension. They have expected him! They have adored him! They have changed the world in order to at least try to follow him!

Still, as time passed, they—we—experienced the same falling away that the Jews experienced after Moses, and again after David and Solomon. Human nature took over. Jesus' second coming was taking too long. God was not meeting our expectations—never mind whether we were meeting *his* expectations. We wanted more immediate gratification. We bickered about teachings and translations. And, OK, if Jesus wasn't going to be here right away, well then, someone had to run things. But who? Why not me? Or what about him? He's better than the other guy; his teachings are easier to stomach.

As with the Hebrew people, divisions rent us: envy, ambition, greed, hatred for the "other." Wars were waged, sometimes even in the name of Jesus, Lord of Peace. Today, we hear talk of end days; entire shelves in bookstores and libraries, not to mention websites, are devoted to novels and prophecies about the end times. People are obsessed with signs and portents, taking Jesus' words and making what they will of them. Much is made of the violent unrest in the Middle East, as if there has not been violent unrest there since the beginning of time.

We have, it seems, given up the joy of discovering Jesus. We have abdicated our duty to know Mary, to understand

what she understood, to feel what she felt. Despite having
every advantage over her because we know the outcome—
we know whom she bore and what he would do—many
of us can barely muster any joy at that birth without two-
months-worth of shopping and trappings to jolt us out of
our stupor.

Even in the midst of their sins and offenses, the Jews were
given a promise by God: there would be a remnant, a number of people who would still believe, still worship, still wait
upon the Lord. Can we not form among us, in each of us, a
remnant for our age, for Christianity? Can we not—as Jesus
warned us that we must—endure and persevere?

If the gospels are to mean anything to us, if our faith has
any real life at all, we must allow ourselves to be stirred, to
feel even just a tremor of pure, crystalline excitement, at
this first verse of the *Magnificat*:

And Mary said, "My soul magnifies the Lord."

Praying and Discussing the *Magnificat* Today

PRAYER

*Mary, I pray that you reach out your hand to me—not the
alabaster hand of a lifeless statue, but the work-hardened,
callused hand of the young girl who had the courage to
say "yes" to God. Touch my head and open my mind to the
magnitude of your experience and what your faith wrought.
Touch my own hands and teach me to open them to others
as Jesus instructed me to do. Touch my breast and open my
heart to your love and God's love so that I may become a
magnification of the Lord in my life. Amen.*

QUESTIONS

1. What is the first image that comes into your mind when you think of Mary? When you think beyond that image, does your perspective change at all?

2. What has most influenced you in your perception of Mary? Church teachings? Movies or television? Art? Scripture? How, if at all, does being aware of these influences impact your thoughts about Mary?

TWO

My Spirit Rejoices

And Mary said, "And my spirit rejoices in God my Savior..."

LUKE 1:47

SETTING THE SCENE

Mary stands on the threshold of the house of Zechariah and Elizabeth. Elizabeth is unable to contain herself, and she embraces her young relative with great exuberance. A few people in this bustling hillside town have started to take notice of the commotion; after all, it is one thing to welcome a visiting family member, but it is another thing to rejoice so dramatically. Neighbors linger outside or stop at their open windows.

What is Elizabeth going on about? they wonder and maybe even murmur to each other. For months she has secluded herself, thanking God for the gift of her pregnancy, caring for herself to protect the precious son that Gabriel promised Zechariah even before the angel visited Mary. The whole village knows the news of Elizabeth's "miracle," but she has been quiet and careful until now. What is it about this girl, this foreign relative from a distant place,

16

that has caused Elizabeth so much excitement? A few of them wonder if she should be making a greater effort to stay calm and collected. She is, they whisper to each other, an old woman, and carrying a child at that. Shouldn't she be resting rather than dancing around this newcomer as though she were some kind of queen?

Standing in the doorway, Mary has her back to the few curious villagers. She is too tired to know or care about their interest as she finds herself falling into Elizabeth's sturdy embrace. Nor is Elizabeth particularly interested in her neighbors or their concerns; she knows what people are and what they think. She knows that they are not always kind; she, of all women, knows this because she has heard their murmurs of sympathy at her barrenness—condemnation, really, clothed in the guise of pity. She knows that they've wondered amongst themselves why God kept her womb empty. Was God punishing her and Zechariah, Levites, of a priestly family? Elizabeth is no fool. She understands that a few of her Judean neighbors have nursed a quiet resentment of Zechariah's love for her despite her childlessness, and that these few, at least, had taken secret pleasure in her shame. Of course, these women were the first to "rejoice" in God taking away the "stain of a barren womb," as one of them put it. Elizabeth had turned a serene smile on them and thanked them.

She does the same now at those neighbors bold enough to stare. They will never know what she knows, never understand the angel's words to her husband, never know the truth about the son in her womb and the one in the womb of this girl wilting in her arms.

As Elizabeth holds her, the past few days, the past few

months, all seem to overwhelm Mary. She feels herself
weakening, feels her whole body bruised by the rough
traveling, her stomach still distressed as it had been for a
few days of late, her bones turned to water in the relief of
seeing Elizabeth, pregnant, aware, waiting. It is all true,
what the angel had said, and now Mary, at first delighted
to see the truth in Elizabeth's body and words, begins to
wonder what it all really means. How can she know? What
will come next?

FOR MARY AND HER JUDEAN FAMILY

Unquestionably, Mary meant the words she had just uttered. Upon seeing Elizabeth embodying Gabriel's promise, Mary's soul did exuberantly magnify the Lord. But
her body was tired. Her mind was weary and struggling to
grasp the reality of her situation. She'd had a plan, and the
plan was to get out of Nazareth and get to Elizabeth. The
plan had worked beautifully. But what now? Now that the
first hurdle had been successfully jumped, Mary was probably fully realizing for the first time just how much her life
had changed—and would continue to change.

Mary, still a child, clung to her older relative, now
perhaps the only friend she had in the world. For though
Mary was a child, she was not a coddled, protected girl.
No girl growing up in Nazareth could be unaware of life's
harshness. She had been told God's intention by Gabriel,
but that did not change the centuries of tradition, based
on Mosaic Law, that would perceive Mary as a lawbreaker,
or worse, an adulterer. How would God accomplish his
purpose in her if people judged her as being in direct op-
position to God's law? How would they understand when

she could hardly comprehend herself what was happening?

Did she wonder if she should just stay exactly where she was, warm and weak in Elizabeth's embrace? Could Zechariah and Elizabeth keep her safe? Would Zechariah understand, upon seeing her, what Elizabeth had understood? Elizabeth may have pondered the same question. Certainly something astonishing and deeply transforming had happened to her husband when he faced Gabriel in the temple. Zechariah had changed in ways she could not fully grasp. Even in his joy at witnessing Gabriel's words come true in her pregnancy, he remained troubled, more serious and anxious than she had ever known him in their long life together. He had been profoundly shocked by his encounter with Gabriel and distressed at the wordlessness that was his punishment. But Elizabeth had been too exultant in finding herself with child, too grateful for God's words through Gabriel, to truly consider what occupied Zechariah's mind night and day.

What was God doing?

Now, with Mary resting in her arms, Elizabeth found herself wondering. There was more here than God granting her and Zechariah the mercy of a son late in life. Merely removing her shame and giving her personal cause to rejoice was not the primary intention of the Almighty. Elizabeth knew now that Zechariah understood this. She knew now because her boy, her John, had leapt in her womb at the sight of Mary. But how would Zechariah respond to the sight of Mary? Would it disturb him even more? Would it help him to understand God's plan? Would he be strong enough? Her husband was older than she, and the past year had carved deeper lines into the face that was so beautiful to her.

She saw him coming along the path to the house. And she felt Mary stir in her arms.

Mary inhaled slowly. This was the man, *from her own family*, who had also spoken with Gabriel. The angel had announced one son to him and another Son to her. Both had heard from Gabriel of the impossible, the miraculous. The angel had made the connection; Gabriel was God's bridge between them, and Gabriel had all but sent her to this house. Wasn't Scripture filled with prophecies about the Son of God, the Messiah, who would be heralded by another, a man also prepared and selected by God?

Suddenly, the confusion and uncertainty that had been only partly banished by Elizabeth's welcome dissipated. Mary felt a surge of power. It was abrupt, as though she been pierced by lightning from the sky, yet allowed to survive and flourish in the living energy. She straightened, feeling her body obey the strength that somehow seemed to be hers. Elizabeth, who'd been bearing her up, now felt Mary's strong, young hands grasp her arms. When Elizabeth looked into her eyes, she saw an exultation that surpassed even that which she and Zechariah had felt at her pregnancy. Elizabeth turned to her husband, standing still, watching with a light in his eyes that seemed to seek Mary's gaze of its own accord. Mary met his look and held it jubilantly.

And Mary said, "And my spirit rejoices in God my Savior."

FOR THE WORLD

Mary's words are, at the same time, profoundly personal and yet reflective of a universal longing—in truth, an expectation—among Israel's children. This phrase may be heard as the spiritual battle cry of the Jews, and although the Jews of the disaspora, and the people of Asia and the Roman Empire, did not hear her utter it, they would experience its reverberations for the rest of human time.

It was a way of saying to the world and its corporeal powers: no matter what you've done to us, no matter how you've persecuted us, no matter how much power you think you have over us, no matter how many of us you crucify and slaughter, no matter how many of our synagogues you destroy, *no matter what you do*, we do not belong to you. We belong to God, and you had better believe that our God will save us. He has done it before, and he will do it again. We are confident of that. Some of us may not live to see it, but we don't doubt for a moment that it will happen. He will see our repentance, he will hear our cries of sorrow and oppression, and he will come. And unless you recognize him, you will be sorry in this life, or the next.

Mary's utterance echoes through the ages. Remember the flood! Remember the tribes that opposed Abraham! Remember the famine! Remember Pharaoh! Remember the Philistines! Remember Holofernes! Remember the Assyrians! Mary's words are a way for her to speak the strength of her people, knowing as all of Israel did, that this strength was not in them, but in the God who made them, and then made them his own.

Mary is also making an observation that would be particularly meaningful to the Jews of her time, a sort of acknowledgment that it is when things look the worst that God will shine through for his people. A member of an occupied nation that over centuries has become painfully familiar with conquerors and servitude, Mary is making a cry for deliverance that would resonate with the Jews. Throughout their existence as a people separated by God from the rest of the world, the Jews turned to God repeatedly when they were most desperate. Mary is using language already used by their prophets.

Habakkuk, a prophet active during the period where the people of Israel had been passed from Assyrian rulers to Babylonian rulers, after describing extensively the miserable situation of the Jews, closed his prophecy with these words: "Yet I will rejoice in the Lord; I will exult in the God of my salvation. God, the Lord, is my strength..." (Habakkuk 3:18–19).

The Jews knew they had something none of the other nations, even those powerful ones that oppressed them, had. They had the repeated promise of God's salvation. No mere man, no mere king, no mere general, was their Savior. God was their Savior! So regardless of how weak and helpless the once great nation of Israel had become, it had the understanding—and the means—of salvation.

Note that Mary did not merely say, "And my spirit rejoices in God." She went on to name God as Savior; even as she pondered Gabriel's declaration that she carried the Son of God, Mary referenced the God of her ancestors. No other nation, regardless of its status in the world, could claim what the Jews claimed: One God who promises and delivers salvation. The Romans, Egyptians, and Greeks had many false deities, to which they assigned specific duties and identities, but these were nothing in the eyes of the Lord Almighty, the One God.

Some thirty-plus years from the moment that Mary uttered this phrase, Jesus himself will confirm his mother's truth when the Samaritan woman at Jacob's well questions Jewish traditions. Jesus responds, "You worship what you do not know; we worship what we know, *for salvation is from the Jews.* But the hour is coming, and is now here, when the true worshipers will worship the Father in spirit and truth, for the Father seeks such as these to worship him" (John 4:22–23, emphasis added).

And Mary said, "And my spirit rejoices in God my Savior."

For Us

The hour that Jesus heralded is the hour that we continue to live in. A long hour, we might think, but perhaps God wants to give us enough time to get this right. How many of us have learned to "worship in spirit and truth"? Or are we not, more often, like Pilate, wondering, "What is truth?"

We can feel a long way away from the teenager on Zechariah's doorstep, boldly declaring that her spirit rejoices in God her Savior. Two thousand years have passed, we tell ourselves; our lives are so much more complicated. We have so many more problems and aggravations than that God-perfected daughter of Nazareth. She grew up in a village of about one hundred families; some of us log one hundred e-mails or texts a day. She was young and innocent; we are hardened and cynical. She was removed from the corruption and changeability of government; we cannot avoid witnessing and experiencing it no matter where we turn.

Of course, these are all rationalizations that we use to comfort ourselves for not following Mary's lead, for not seeking and worshiping God in spirit and truth. Are we so convinced that our lives are so far beyond the pale of Mary's life? Can we be that arrogant, to think that we understand more about the world than did the child who was the mother of God? Do we seriously judge ourselves to have more problems than Mary did?

Yes, she would return to a village of less than one hundred families; and every single member of every single one of them would have their condemning eyes fixed on her growing belly; she did not have the luxury of anonymity that so many of us enjoy. Yes, she was young and innocent, but she faced the possibility of being stoned for committing adultery when she had not; most of our children don't make it to college without a sexual experience, and no one bats an eye. No, she probably didn't save for the future and worry about money for retirement because she was too busy, with her family and village, securing enough food and shelter for the day. Nor did many people in Nazareth live long enough to "retire." Granted, she did not experience the corruption of Jewish government because it had been so long since the Jews had been able to truly and independently govern themselves. And, no, Mary did not face the threat of global terrorism; she faced it in her own land from Roman soldiers, other enemies of the Jews, and the bandits who terrorized travelers in the wilderness places of Palestine.

Mary had all the same worries and difficulties that we do, and quite likely more. But she came from a people who could never forget their heritage, their God. Mary's spirit could rejoice in God her Savior during the most challenging and, eventually, grievous and frightening of circumstances *because* of those very circumstances! Mary—and the children of Israel—knew that they needed God; thus their spirits could never stray completely from God. It would be Jews who were close to God's Spirit who would recognize in Jesus the home for their own spirit to rest and rejoice.

And Mary said, "And my spirit rejoices in God my Savior."

Praying and Discussing the *Magnificat* Today

Prayer

Mary, my own spirit is so often careworn and weary. Some days I feel so far from the strong, young girl that you were, so far from the teachings of the Son you would bear. Let me bear witness to your courage. Let me be strengthened by your strength. Let my small sparks of faith be inflamed by the enduring flames of faith that consumed your whole life. Help me to lift my spirit just enough to recognize God my Savior! Help me to lift my spirit just enough to join with God's Spirit! Help me to lift my spirit just enough to be caught in the upwelling of God's truth and to worship God with rejoicing and gratitude. Amen.

Questions

1. If you were in Mary's sandals, could you rejoice in your situation? If you were in Elizabeth's and Zechariah's sandals, would you be able to rejoice in welcoming Mary into your home?

2. How do the words "God my Savior" impact you? When you think of your Savior, who comes to mind: Father, Son, Spirit, or Triune Godhead? How have you been saved by the Savior, and how does your spirit rejoice in that salvation?

THREE

Call Me Blessed

*And Mary said, "For he has looked with favor on the lowliness
of his servant. Surely, from now on all generations
will call me blessed."* Luke 1:48

SETTING THE SCENE

Mary is now speaking not only to Elizabeth but to Zechariah as well. She may not fully realize that more of the Judean villagers are gathering close enough to hear. While they may have been perplexed to note Elizabeth's uncharacteristically exuberant reaction to this young visitor, they are now truly surprised to see Zechariah's joy at beholding the young girl. For months now their old friend has not been himself. Of course, who *could* be himself after seeing a vision in the Jerusalem temple?! Not only was Zechariah touched by God's angel; he was struck dumb by the encounter!

Elizabeth watches her husband's reaction to Mary's presence with great happiness, for she sees the burden that he has carried since that day in the temple lift from his countenance. The confusion, the bemusement, is gone, and as Zechariah stares at their young relative with a dawning

understanding, Elizabeth herself begins to realize that
what is happening here is beyond her ability to fully comprehend. Their observant neighbors have no idea what this
portends.

Only Elizabeth knows the true reason for Zechariah's
silence: that he doubted the angel's declaration that she
would bear a son. Her husband, always quick to speak his
mind, even in the presence of God's angel, had questioned
the heavenly being! He had written down all the details of
that encounter so that she could understand his silence
and to provide a record of what had happened. She had
been terrified when she first read this account. *What have
you done?* she'd been unable to keep herself from asking,
still not fully understanding that he could not, would not,
answer her. He had only stared back at her, pleading with
his eyes that she understand. *How could I **not** question
Gabriel's words?* he seemed to ask his wife. What the angel
predicted—that she would become pregnant and bear a
son—was impossible! How could he not question this?

She had turned away from him, frightened and confused. To be punished by an angel was like being punished by the Almighty himself! What would become of
Zechariah? Would he be forgiven? Would he ever be
able to speak again? How would they explain this to their
neighbors, to the other priestly families? At first they
would believe simply that he'd seen a vision, but how long
before they would suspect that he had done something
wrong, something to offend the Almighty God? How long
before they would avoid him, avoid her, begin to think him
cursed and not blessed? *Couldn't you keep your tongue still
just once?* she had wanted to cry in frustration.

But then she found herself with child.

The first part of the angel's promise was fulfilled, and Elizabeth had come to believe that the second part would come true as well: that Zechariah would regain his voice when their son was born.

Now, seeing him move to grasp Mary's hands in his own, his face clear of any lingering distress, she is as certain as the leaping child in her womb that the Lord their God is with them.

Though witnessing Elizabeth's pregnancy and hearing her words of greeting and blessing have given Mary much comfort, it is Zechariah whose eyes reflect their shared knowledge. He alone knows what Elizabeth is only beginning to sense. That the Son in Mary's womb and the son in Elizabeth's are linked in a way that will fulfill God's plan from all past ages for all future ages. Here in this small house, in this small village, in these close hills, in this chosen family, God's words are being fulfilled. Mary steps softly into Zechariah's embrace.

For Mary and her Judean Family

This encounter at the home of Zechariah and Elizabeth, these first precious moments and hours, is the bridge between the personal and the universal. It is during this time that these three people, the older couple and their young relative, begin to understand the enormity of what is happening, the marvel of God's plan. They are passing through the last moments when they will rejoice solely in their own personal happiness, the very human pride and joy of bringing new life into the world. It is the last time these too-old-to-be-parents parents will consider the energetic boy in Elizabeth's womb their own. It is the last time Mary will consider herself simply a young relative coming to share the joy of motherhood with her distant family. Each of them has understood to some extent that their coming together is much more momentous than a familial celebration, but in the next minutes and hours and days, they will eventually surrender what is so very personal and accept that God has chosen them as the vehicles by which he will transform the world.

Mary's entire *Magnificat* is a proclamation blending the personal and the universal. In the personal aspect, hers is very much like the prayer of Hannah, the mother of the great prophet Samuel. Though Hannah is more a precursor of Elizabeth, and Samuel of John the Baptist, Hannah's proclamation upon discovering that God had kept his promise and that she was pregnant is similar in many ways to Mary's *Magnificat*.

Hannah began, "My heart exults in the Lord; my strength is exalted in my God. My mouth derides my enemies because I rejoice in my victory. The Lord makes poor and makes rich; he brings low, he also exalts" (1 Samuel 2:1, 7).

When Hannah thought herself to be barren, she prayed ceaselessly for a son, promising to dedicate her male child to God if her prayer was answered. In this too she prayed with words very much like those used by Gabriel when instructing Zechariah as to how John should be raised and live his life. Both sons, in God's plan, were promised as ones set aside, or Nazarites; they will not drink wine or spirits; they will not live a "normal" life among their kin. They will live in the wild as God guides them. They will belong to God.

At the birth of John, Zechariah's prophetic song of

praise will also incorporate many of the images and words of Hannah's prayer. Zechariah, a priest, would have been well aware of Hannah's prayer through his knowledge of Scripture, and it is quite possible that Mary's words also drew on the prayer. History exists in God, and without God there is no history; the circle formed by the Old and New Testaments provides ample evidence of this.

Sarah, Rachel, Hannah: Scripture abounds with stories of beloved or aging wives who cannot get pregnant until God "looked favorably on me and took away the disgrace I have endured among my people" (Luke 1:25), as Elizabeth proclaimed, seemingly for all of them. Now we find her, perhaps the eldest of the miraculously pregnant wives, meeting the young and pregnant virgin, the one who is not yet a true wife and who needed no man to become pregnant. As Mary, Zechariah, and Elizabeth come to comprehend more fully what is unfolding, they will also realize that they have been chosen as God's agents in this soon-to-be-completed circle.

The personal delight in Mary's comment about being called blessed can be starkly contrasted some thirty years later with the cold and somewhat startling observation of the Son who makes her blessed when he describes the universal nature of that blessing. After a woman in the crowd raised her voice and said to him, "Blessed is the womb that bore you and the breasts that nursed you!" he said, "Blessed rather are those who hear the word of God and obey it!" (Luke 11:27–28).

Mary, Elizabeth, and Zechariah are experiencing, and will continue to experience over the next three-and-a-half decades, all degrees of this spectrum. From the intensely

personal, ordinary, human miracle of conceiving and bearing children, they will move toward the wrenching sacrifice
required of them by God's eternal plan. All generations,
indeed, will call Mary blessed, but can she now fully know
what that will cost her?

And Mary said, "For he has looked with favor on the
lowliness of his servant. Surely, from now on all generations will call me blessed."

For the World

Mary is not kidding when she observes that God has
looked with favor on the lowliness of his servant. For in the
eyes of the world, this young, unknown girl is, indeed, no-
body. But God does not see with the eyes of the world, and
through Mary, God is about to make that truth abundantly
known.

Still, Mary is humbly admitting a worldly fact in, as we
now say, "real time." While her parents and neighbors in
Nazareth may know her as a good girl, perhaps exception-
ally so, she is not in any visible, human way extraordinary.
She is not preparing to marry out of her village, perhaps
to a wealthier or more successful man living in a city closer to Jerusalem. Her family is not considered among the
elders or leaders. She does not come from an important
city. Nazareth at the time is thought to have had no more
than five hundred residents. There is no indication that her
parents are wealthy or powerful in any way. Even in prog-
eny, they do not seem to be blessed; neither Scripture nor
tradition suggests that Mary had brothers. Certainly, they
were not known in Jerusalem or among those who ruled
the temple; Nazareth was considered so much an outpost

of civilization that much later, Jesus will be dismissed because no one of any religious consequence could possibly come from Nazareth.

In the wider world, the Jews themselves were a small, despised, fractured people. Rome considered them a nettlesome aggravation useful only for what taxes could be extorted from them. Historians have speculated that Pilate was later sent to govern Palestine as either a punishment or a test of his mettle. The Jews had no real leaders, no independently powerful men of their own to contend on the world stage. Caesars ruled the world, Alexanders ruled the world, Ptolemys ruled the world, Herods ruled the world. Jews were not even considered capable of ruling their own small, difficult patch of the world. Clearly, the idea of a Jewish virgin from Nazareth bearing the One who would rule all worlds would have been inconceivable to Jew or Gentile at the time.

Could God have set it up any better to demonstrate to the world his affinity to "look with favor on the lowliness of his servant"(s)?

Mary's humility cannot be overemphasized, and through it, God is sending the world a message, or maybe, a reminder. Already, for thousands of years, he has plucked the unnotable out of their seemingly wretched circumstances and made of them judges and kings and prophets and leaders. Noah was an object of ridicule. Abraham was rejected by his family. Jacob was the smaller, weaker twin. Joseph was despised by his brothers. Moses was saved from certain death by his enslaved mother, who lovingly laid him in a basket among the reeds of the Nile River. David was thought to be so young and useless that his father almost forgot to present him to Samuel. Yet all of these, and more, had women—also considered of no import by worldly standards—who bore them, loved them, tried to protect them: Sarah, Rebecca, Rachel, Moses' mother and sister, Hannah.

Why then, should the world have been so surprised when God chose another seemingly lowly servant to bear and raise his Son, a Son who would preach and embody the very nature of humility?

And Mary said, "For he has looked with favor on the lowliness of his servant. Surely, from now on all generations will call me blessed."

For Us

For us, God's choice of Mary to fulfill his plan is both inspiring and a little scary. Inspiring because if God chose someone who appeared to the world to be so unextraordinary, imagine what he might have in store for us! And scary because if God chose someone who appeared to the world to be so unextraordinary, imagine what he might *expect* of us!

It is easy to try to use our ordinariness—our lowliness—to hide from God. (Easy, but futile, as we all eventually learn.) We are so weak, so bland, so uninfluential, how can we possibly act boldly in the service of God? we ask ourselves. How can we, with so many mundane responsibilities and daily pressures, find a way to put all that aside and devote ourselves to learning and doing God's will? What if we don't have enough money? What if we get sick or exhausted? What if God's work requires us to put aside another obligation? What if we alienate a friend, coworker, or family member? Surely God does not expect so much of us?

Mary and, for that matter, Zechariah and Elizabeth, refute all these protestations. Not only does God call us and seek us to answer this call, he seeks us to have the faith we need to have in order to respond. Mary did not ask Gabriel whether he would keep her Nazareth neighbors from maligning, or even stoning, her. She did not question whether he would arrange for the means and the permission she would need to travel to Elizabeth and Zechariah in the Judean hill country. She did not ask him if he might next go to her parents and Joseph and explain the whole thing to them for her. She did not wonder aloud how she, a poor girl from Nazareth, would be able to raise and protect and teach the Son of God.

Mary, the poor lowly servant, had none of the resources, education, services, or support that are available to us on a daily basis in this wildly successful country of ours. But she had something that we, caught up in our busy lives, sadly lack. She had a deep, unwavering faith. She simply believed in a truth that her Son would later confirm for the masses who heard him: that God would provide for her needs while she went about doing his business.

What a leap of faith that would be for us with the weighty baggage of our family dysfunctions, our career demands, our spousal spats, our health insurance concerns, our *health* concerns, our retirement savings, our monthly budgets, our worries about aging parents, our church commitments, our three meals a day to procure and prepare!

How much humility does it require for us to become lowly, and thus blessed?

And Mary said, "For he has looked with favor on the lowliness of his servant. Surely, from now on all generations will call me blessed."

Praying and Discussing the *Magnificat* Today

Prayer

Mary, when I stop and think about the faith you demonstrated as such a young woman and throughout your life, I am left in awe. To understand that your magnificent faith grew from your humility, from your abiding sense of your own lowliness, almost makes me want to give up on myself! But I can't! Because there you are, standing in Elizabeth and Zechariah's doorway, alone, forever separated by God's plan from those who loved you and thought they knew you best, forever separated from any hope of a "normal" life. There you are, standing in my doorway, showing me the way forward, beckoning me to take at least a small step in your direction. I don't think I am capable of making the leap you made; but with your help, I will strive to take that first step. Amen.

Questions

1. When you call someone "blessed," what do you mean? That they have a particularly good life or have had a wonderful thing happen to them? Would you consider someone "blessed" if they were, by all outward appearances, poor and humble, with few worldly goods or little influence?

2. Do you ever feel that God has "looked with favor" upon you? If so, what are/were the circumstances that made you feel that way?

FOUR

Holy Is His Name

And Mary said, "For the Mighty One has done great things
for me, and holy is his Name." LUKE 1:49

SETTING THE SCENE

Elizabeth begins to beckon her husband and Mary deeper into the house, where they can have some privacy from the curious villagers. The inner room is dim, and they will have more protection from the hot sun; she knows herself how punishing the sun can be, especially during early pregnancy. In fact, now that Elizabeth has had a little more time to observe, she can see that Mary looks thin and worn out. The journey could not have been an easy one, and surely the poor child must have been anxious. The sooner she comes in to rest, the better.

But Zechariah surprises Elizabeth. Instead of helping her draw Mary inside, her husband smiles and gently takes his wife's hand. Then with one arm still around Mary, he draws both women out into the small yard, facing the neighbors who continue to watch the unfolding scene. Elizabeth resists at first, using her eyes to silently communicate with her husband as only a couple who have been

38

together for many years can. *What are you doing?* her eyes ask him. *Can't you see she's exhausted? This is not the business of the whole village.*

But for the first time since he returned from the temple, her old Zechariah—the impetuous, sure-of-himself Zechariah—looks back at her, his own eyes lit with excitement and commanding her to follow. Elizabeth sees that his confidence has returned, and the few neighbors who are watching closely see it as well. They murmur and come closer, a few of them smiling uncertainly in anticipation of what Zechariah intends. They see that he has returned to himself, and that alone is reason to be pleased. Reluctantly, Elizabeth follows, though she feels distressed when her husband deliberately turns Mary toward the people as if to introduce her. Why can't Zechariah see that the last thing the girl needs right now is some kind of public presentation? She does not even know herself what is in store for her; none of them do.

News spreads quickly in their village, and the news that Zechariah has come back to them is no exception. Others start to join their near neighbors, and Elizabeth is somewhat relieved to see that they seem more attentive to her husband than to Mary, who has now put herself in their hands for help and protection. It is no wonder, Elizabeth realizes, that they are interested in Zechariah's transformation. He was a leader among them, of a priestly family, and his silence and preoccupation since his time of service in the temple has been a subject of much debate among them. Elizabeth has heard their whispers. And those she hasn't heard, she has imagined. None of them have denied believing what they've been told: that Zechariah saw a vision in the temple.

But Elizabeth knows they speculate. What did the priest see? Why is he stricken silent? If God had sent him a good vision, a gift, then why doesn't he speak of it? Does he choose this silence because of the magnitude of his vision, or has God rendered him without speech? Where is the priest's characteristic good humor and courage in proclaiming God's Scripture? And if God has done this to him, the boldest among them wonder, could it be in punishment? Is Zechariah still worthy to be a priest?

Elizabeth knows her neighbors, the villagers. She has never been as open to them as her husband, for she is quiet by nature, and her lifelong barrenness has taught her caution. She knows how people will talk. She knows how easily envy and superstition can stir a good person to malice. In her many years among these people, none have said an unpleasant word to her; yet she's heard the quiet, secret condemnation of some among them. God has made her barren! She must have some unknown guilt! Poor Zechariah, to be a priest without sons or even a daughter who could marry and perhaps carry on with sons of her own! None of them have ever turned anything but a smiling face in her direction, but Elizabeth is wise. She knows what some of them think. She has few friends and trusts only her husband.

This was why when Gabriel's declaration came true, she secluded herself. She was not quick to rejoice with those who had so avidly witnessed her shame. And though she had pitied her husband his silence and uncharacteristic solitude, she had not been sorry about it. For once he was content to leave the world outside their walls, with all its whispers and problems, to itself. For once he was more interested in searching the Scriptures than discussing them. She had secretly enjoyed having him with her, quietly, just the two of them. She had taken hidden pleasure in being the only one to know about Gabriel and his precious words.

But now she sees that Zechariah is forcing an end to their peaceful days, their blessed solitude. Not only is he turning back to the people, he is bringing her and Mary before them as well. She can see that they are all waiting for Zechariah to, finally, speak.

But Zechariah does not speak.

For Mary and her Judean Family

Mary does feel weary, but now this feeling is only in her body. Her spirit has lifted. God has given her the strength to take this next step. He has given her the foundation of Zechariah and Elizabeth, both from God's priestly line, and he has set her on the foundation of their own home. She understands that she no longer belongs to herself and that God has delivered her to these people so that she can be the means through which he will deliver them. Mary may not have the words to express this on her own, but she knows it in her bones and her womb, and she knows that God will give her the words.

This is the last time in her prayer of praise that Mary will speak of the personal. In this single verse, she makes the transformation from a girl experiencing a miracle to the woman God is giving for all time to the world. Again, this is very similar to the pattern of Hannah's prayer of praise when she leaves her son, Samuel, to the service of God, as she promised she would when God answered her plea for a son. Hannah first rejoices in her own, private triumph before moving on to an exuberant and universal praise of God's greatness and power. The personal sense of ascendency in both her prayer and Mary's is echoed throughout Scripture in the words of women whom God favors with children.

Leah, Jacob's first and sadly unloved, unattractive wife, repeatedly declared her victory over her lovely sister Rachel for no other reason than Leah's fertility. Leah loudly rejoiced each time she—and even her maid—bore a son to Jacob, even naming her boys to reflect her triumphant fecundity. Her words sound much like Hannah's and Mary's, never more so than when she bears the third and all-important son, Judah. Leah "conceived again and bore a son, and said, 'This time I will praise the Lord'; therefore she named him Judah" (Genesis 29:35).

But whereas several women in the Bible—Leah, Sarah, even Rachel eventually—do not progress much beyond the almost gloating personal praise of God for opening their wombs, Hannah shows herself to be the mother of a prophet, citing God's mighty works as her prayer continues. She recognizes and strongly declaims that God's power is far greater and has more important objectives than merely granting the personal prayer of a seemingly barren wife. Hannah praises God's universal promise to all his people, a promise that her son, Samuel, will, at God's urging, advance by anointing David king and thus establishing the genealogy from which Jesus' human parents will emerge twenty-eight generations later.

It should be no surprise, then, that this thread of universal, eternal praise will be continued by David, a prophet in his own right, who will frequently refer to God's coming Messiah. The psalms, meant for all humankind and not only for a few rejoicing individuals or families, are replete with such concise Messianic references: "He sent redemption to his people; he has commanded his covenant forever. Holy and awesome is his name" (Psalm 111:9). In a single verse, David extends and envisions the implementation of Hannah's praise song—Jesus *is* God's covenant and redemption forever—while offering what is essentially the prequel to the third verse of Mary's *Magnificat*.

This is the last verse in which Mary will refer to herself. Up until now, there have been three "my"s and two "me"s. From here on in, Mary's entire focus will be on what God is accomplishing for his people. The *Magnificat* now moves from an expression of personal awe and thanksgiving to the consummation of Jewish history, the "groaning" as St. Paul would later put it, of God's chosen people waiting for this birth. Elizabeth and, especially, Zechariah, recognize this in Mary's words. The others will hear her with only a hazy comprehension; later some will remember…and understand.

The attention of those in the Judean village is fixed on Zechariah. But it is the young girl standing beside him who speaks.

And Mary said, "For the Mighty One has done great things for me, and holy is his name."

FOR THE WORLD

Few people living in the world at the time would listen to Mary's words, and only a few more would hear them repeated in their own time. Almost all of them would be Jews. But as with many of the verses of the *Magnificat*, the import of this one would have terrified the powerful and deeply comforted the despised and the captive, the used and the abused, the struggling and the defeated, the frightened and the lowly. Mary's prophetic final combination of the personal and the universal in this verse would have been chilling to the leaders and oppressors of the time, whether they were the Jewish ruling class, the false tetrarchs Herod and his brothers, or the Romans.

Mary's declaration is a clarion call to the oppressed of the world. On the personal end, for whom has the Mighty One done great things? Not for greedy, lustful Herod and his lackey brothers, who have gained their wealth from the broken backs of the people that Rome has allowed them to rule and exploit. Not for the Pharisees, scribes, Sadducees, and lawyers, most of whom maintain their positions and grow wealthy at the pleasure of Rome and who, as her Son will later say, "neglect justice and the love of God" and "are like unmarked graves and people walk over them without realizing it" and "load people with burdens hard to bear, and you yourselves do not lift a finger to ease them" (Luke 11:42, 44, 46), and "You are wrong because you know neither the scriptures nor the power of God" (Matthew 22:29). Certainly not for the Romans, who with cold calculation brutally oppress and even crucify those who defy them in even the smallest way.

No, the Mighty One has done great things, on the personal level, for *Mary*, a girl unknown to any of those who lay claim to worldly power or possessions. Imagine what this meant—had they only known—for all of those living under Roman rule at the time! A Power existed and was coming into the world so much greater than anything the world had thus far experienced in human terms. Not only that, but this Power was *on their side*, on the side of the lowly, the forgotten, the voiceless. This Power, God, God Incarnate, was not coming for the temporal powers of the world, but for each individual, starting with Mary, the one chosen by God to bring God.

At the same time, as utterly as the coming of God would transform persons, there would be a universal transformation. This was particularly relevant to Jews who were not in Palestine, Jews who were part of the diaspora. By the time Mary came on the scene, Jews had been scattered all over the known world. For centuries, Jews had been taken captive or had moved throughout the Middle East and into Europe for political and economic reasons. Many had been captured, brought to new cities, and simply stayed there once their captors fell out of power. From the universal perspective, Mary is calling out to these Jews all over the world, as well as to the Gentiles and Greeks who would soon be brought into the family of God by Jesus.

Holy is his name, she is telling them, and you are all about to witness just how holy, just how powerful. Your God has not forgotten you, she is telling everyone in the world who yearns for God, for salvation, even those who are not Jewish and do not yet even understand how intently their spirits are searching for God. All you in the world who are discontented, she is crying out, all you who are persecuted and debased and despised, lift up your faces and listen to my words. Your time is coming; it is upon you.

And Mary said, "For the Mighty One has done great things for me, and holy is his name."

FOR US

What do Mary's words mean for us? After all, we know
that Jesus came, and we know how the world was changed.

But do we?

For us, Luke 1:49 is not so much an announcement, as it
was for the people of Mary's time, but a reminder. It is a call
to turn back to the God who has done mighty things for us
and whose name is holy. Wait, come the protests, we don't
need to turn back to God because we haven't turned away.

Haven't we?

Do we assure ourselves that we haven't turned away
from God because, well, we attend church, we contribute to the basket, and we drop a few cans of soup into
the box for the hungry? Mary is reminding us that God
in the world is not a routine thing, not part of the daily
grind. God in the world is something magnificent, something that should take our breath away, whether we live
today or lived two thousand years ago. Perhaps one of the
most discomfiting differences between us and the Jews of
Mary's world is that they *knew* they were in need of the
Messiah. They yearned for God's Savior. They waited and
prayed and hoped every day for the Christ of God. They
searched Scripture avidly for words about God's promise
of a Messiah.

Many of us are much more complacent. Sure, God came
into the world and is still here...somewhere. How often do
we echo Mary's words: "the Mighty One has done great
things for me"? Do we count our blessings with awe and
gratitude? Do we attribute our blessings to God at all?
Mary's humility is key here. She takes credit for none of
what has happened to her. We don't see her bragging about

how good she is, how appropriate it is that God has chosen her. She doesn't tell Elizabeth that she always suspected she was destined for something wonderful and miraculous. There is no ego in Mary, no sense of her own self-importance. A mere child, she knows that she owes everything to God; more important, she knows that we all owe everything to God.

And Mary said, "For the Mighty One has done great things for me, and holy is his name."

Praying and Discussing the *Magnificat* Today

PRAYER

Mary, thank you for reminding me of the two truths that should shape my world: God has done great things for me, and God has done great things in and for the world. It is so easy for me to rejoice in what I see as my successes and lament what I see as my failures. It is so easy for me to celebrate the great events in the world and become mired in the tragedies. It is so easy for me to see everything through the very narrow prism of my own perspective. Blessed mother and humble girl, continue to help me turn my face always to the Holy One, always acknowledging my need and his mightiness. Amen.

QUESTIONS

1. What great things has the Mighty One done for you personally? What great things has God done in the world? Do you see any parallels in how God acts in your life and in the world?

2. Do you ever feel that God is calling upon you, as he did with Mary, to express his presence in your personal life in a more universal or global way? How does this make you feel? Challenged? Joyful? Terrified? Why?

FIVE

Mercy for Generations

*And Mary said, "His mercy is for those who fear him
from generation to generation."* LUKE 1:50

SETTING THE SCENE

Most likely Mary has never spoken to more than one or two people at a time before. She has never had a real conversation except with the members of her family and a few of the girls she grew up with, and even those were mostly over once it became known that she had been promised in marriage. She has hardly said more than a few words to Joseph, her betrothed. Never before had she even considered speaking aloud to a group of people. Nor has anyone expected her to; indeed, she would be thought forward or disrespectful to speak to strangers or anyone outside her immediate circle.

And yet these people are watching her so avidly—some still with suspicion shadowing their faces, some with eyes glowing expectantly. Most of them simply look astounded. For this is not normal—a young girl, a stranger, a distant relation of the quiet, cautious Elizabeth and the priest Zechariah, to be speaking in such a loud, clear voice to people who do not know her, most of them her elders! It seems to them that the girl—from Nazareth, of all places!—is speaking words that only Zechariah should speak. He is, after all, their priest; until he was struck dumb, he could hardly be stopped from speaking! Has he given her these words? Written them down so that she could tell all of them what is in his mind? But then, why would he not have given the words to Elizabeth? She, his wife and also of priestly lineage, could have spoken for him long before now. Why wait for this girl?

And yet the girl does not seem to be speaking for Zechariah, though he stands beside her beaming with joy as he has not since returning from the temple, silenced, so many months ago. Far from trying to silence her as an elder should, he is keen to hear every word of what she will say. Even the news of Elizabeth's astonishing pregnancy did not appear to give him as much delight as the words of this girl.

Look at her! After traveling for days on the dangerous way from Nazareth to their village, she should be weary, but she seems to glow with the words inside her. It is as if she cannot keep herself from letting them pour out. The words are familiar; they have heard—and some of them, even read—the words of Moses and the songs of David and the promises of their prophets. But this girl, Mary, is using them in a different way. They don't understand; they gather closer to her.

What amazes Mary more than any of this is that she is not afraid. This long, long day feels like it will never end, and yet her strength is renewed. With Zechariah beside her and Elizabeth's strong, warm presence just slightly behind her, she feels full to overflowing. She understands that she came here for more than mere confirmation that the angel spoke truly of Elizabeth's pregnancy. She came here, also, for this.

For Mary and her Judean Family

For Zechariah and Elizabeth, Mary's words awakened emotions and hopes they had not dared to nurture, or even to admit to themselves when Gabriel's promise was fulfilled in Elizabeth's womb. They both knew that Gabriel had described the work God had prepared for the son he would give them, and they both knew that this work, to prepare the world for the Messiah, could only mean that God was preparing to send his Messiah. But to know now that Mary—*their* Mary—would bear the Messiah set them both trembling. And to hear her speak the ancient words in such a new, bold way was almost more than they could bear.

Though both Elizabeth and her husband heard the echo of God's words in Mary's message and they saw the shadow of his presence in her very being, their reactions were different. Zechariah was beside himself, exultant. He knew that some of the villagers listening were surprised that he let this young girl speak for him. Speak for him? She was not speaking for him, for Zechariah was beginning to understand that this woman would never need to speak for another. God was speaking through her! And from now on, if God ever granted him speech again, Zechariah would speak—not for her, but of her. And his son would speak of her Son. Zechariah felt that if the angel had not struck him dumb, Mary's words—Mary herself!—would have accomplished the same end.

Elizabeth had not taken as long as her husband to discern Mary's power, to understand the meaning of Mary arriving at their door. Indeed, the child in Elizabeth's womb had taught her from the first moment she saw Mary. Elizabeth knew more fully in her body than in her mind what was happening to the three of them, to Israel, and to the world. And she trembled not only in excitement but in fear. She trembled as a mother will tremble, as her young relative standing before them all would soon tremble. Elizabeth trembled at the power and majesty of God. Elizabeth trembled at the overwhelming truth that God's promise would be fulfilled among them, through them. And Elizabeth trembled because she sensed within herself, at the very core of her being, what the cost of God's sacrifice would be to them. Elizabeth's hands splayed open over her belly as if to protect her own son from what was coming.

Mary's hands extended outward to the people in the yard, to Zechariah, to Israel. She knew that her words would not be strange to them, though they would wonder why she spoke them. They were unable to understand, to see, and Mary felt that some of them never would. They would have all been familiar with Moses' record of God's words to the consecrated people of Israel just before giving them his Ten Commandments: "For I the Lord your God am a jealous God, punishing children for the iniquity of parents, to the third and fourth generation of those who reject me, *but showing steadfast love to the thousandth generation of those who love me and keep my commandments*" (Exodus 20:5–6, emphasis added).

Mary knew that the rugged, careworn people here understood intimately the God of the first part, the jealous

God, the God who punished iniquity. Even more so, her own people in the region of Galilee to the north knew that stern God. But Mary felt that the God inside her was coming to remind them of, and to show them as never before, his true Self, the Self they longed to see and experience: the God who demonstrated compassion through second chances, who expressed love to Moses and the Israelites in the desert by beginning the second part of his message with the word *but.*

And Mary said, "His mercy is for those who fear him from generation to generation."

FOR THE WORLD

Many generations after Moses recorded God's threat and promise, King David also emphasized the understanding and mercy of God in the Psalms. By the time David was writing, it was painfully clear that the people would fail God again and again and again. (We still do.) David, who also failed despite being chosen by God, had a great deal of time and experience to consider when it came to the subject of human failure. He came to a conclusion, often expressed in the Psalms, that many people still struggle with: if God's mercy was not stronger than God's anger, no one could stand. Few people living at the time of Moses, or at the time of David, or at the time of Zechariah and Elizabeth, or in our time, claimed to be perfect before God. Jesus and Paul will soon suggest that no one is perfect before God. And yet God gives us more chances, more time, more ways to experience forgiveness and grow closer to him, and kinder to one another. Human nature, in all its weakness and tendency to sin, is about the most perfect argument for God's mercy. David knew this, and so the Psalms are among the most comforting words in the Bible. Many of them serve the dual purpose of reaching back into Jewish history and forward to the Messiah: "*But* the steadfast love of the Lord is from everlasting to everlasting on those who fear him, and his righteousness to children's children to those who keep his covenant and remember to do his commandments" (Psalm 103:17–18). Once again we have the *but*, signifying not only the power of God *but* his mercy. That Mary chooses, or is given, words much like those written by Moses and David is significant. Everything may seem the same, even worse than in the past, *but* things are changing.

Yes, Mary is telling the world, you have all perceived God's power and punishment moving through your world until the present, *but* now God is about to show you something different. Punishment and anger are fading. Should you fear God? Yes, *but* what you should fear is the loss of him. Do not fear knowing him, *but* fear missing him. Fear not only angering him, *but* fear hurting him. Fear not only disobeying him, *but* fear disappointing him. Listen! Mary tells the world. The Almighty is ready to shower forth mercy upon the earth and to make steadfast love his prime mover in the world. You are being given still another chance. And this is the One.

And Mary said, "His mercy is for those who fear him from generation to generation."

FOR US

For many of us, depending upon how we were raised and how we responded to how we were raised, God can seem to be one extreme or the other. If we were raised in a traditional or strict religious home, we may have a hard time shaking the idea that God is mostly the punishing God we often see in the Old Testament, waiting for us to go wrong, disgusted at the state of the world (or maybe it's just that most of us are disgusted at the state of the world). Deep within us, we feel that God chucked Adam and Eve out of the garden for good reason, and no one's ever getting back in.

We may have been taught a number of rituals and traditions that seemed to confirm that conviction, or we may have been taught in a manner that made us believe that God could never really be happy with us. I can remember being terrified when told as a seven-year-old that if I touched the host with my teeth while swallowing the Holy Eucharist, God would be furious. I can also remember kneeling in the darkened church before my first confession, rapidly repeating the phrases I was supposed to say because I'd heard that if I got it wrong, the priest would be horrified. And if I horrified the priest, imagine what God might think of me.

These can be amusing party stories as we tell ourselves we are completely over such ideas. And, intellectually, we may well be. But have such terrors been totally purged from our hearts and our guts? We may no longer be afraid of the priest behind the darkened screen—quite often because we no longer go to confession, an avoidance that is as much a reaction to early experiences as is going constantly and being filled with shame—but have we lost that dread of God?

There is a difference between fearing God and dreading God. Jesus is that difference. Jesus taught us that to fear God means to be awed, to venerate, to be overwhelmed, to revere, to respect. Jesus personified God's mercy. He showed us that fear is pointless if it does not motivate us to want to do right by God and to be right before God. What should make us fear sin is that sin is painful to God. While dread festers and destroys, fear—the "good" fear that Jesus inculcates—increases our love for God and our desire to be closer to him. If we understand that we are to fear in this way, we understand that God's mercy is already ours.

So when Jesus' young mother spoke these words about the fear of God, she was turning Jewish history on its ear and redefining the concepts of fear and mercy. Mary was speaking to us, too, and there was no *but* in her statement. God, from this time forward, would be all about *and*, for the whole world was about to be added to the fear and mercy equation.

And Mary said, "His mercy is for those who fear him from generation to generation."

Praying and Discussing the *Magnificat* Today

Prayer

Mary, forgive me for sometimes wondering what you—a sinless, pure girl—really know about the fear of God. When were you ever in need of God's mercy as I seem to be constantly in need of it? What fault did you show to God, while I demonstrate my failings on a daily basis? Still, even then, before you could fully comprehend what your life had become, you were the mediator. The one who stood calmly between God and the rest of us, the one who would stand be-

side Jesus as he went out into the world, the one who would hold Jesus' precious body in your arms when he was born and after he was crucified. Mary, forgive me for wondering how you could know anything about the fear and mercy of God! You experienced it every day of your life. Intercede for me, Mary, that I may better know the fruits of fearing God well and the peace of embracing God's mercy! Amen.

QUESTIONS

1. Do you think Mary was afraid? If so, do you think she was afraid of God? Did she come to fear losing her Son when she began to fully understand what would happen to him? How do you think she communicated with God through all this?

2. When you honestly explore your feelings, do you fear God? If so, how? What are your greatest fears relating to God? How does your understanding of God's mercy impact your fear?

SIX

The Proud Scattered

And Mary said, "He has shown strength with his arm; he has scattered the proud in the thoughts of their hearts." LUKE 1:51

SETTING THE SCENE

Word had spread quickly in the village, and a few men now joined their wives in front of the house of Zechariah and Elizabeth. Had it been the house of a lesser man, had it not been the house of a man whom God had seemed to both punish with silence and reward with an impossible child, had it not been the house of a man who had spoken in the past at great length to all of Scripture, explaining concepts some of them would have never understood, had it not been the house of a man who was known for kindness and unfailing generosity, had it not been the house of a man about whom they once felt they knew everything but now suspected they knew nothing, they would have ignored the words being spoken all over the hill-country town: that Zechariah's young relative, a mere girl, was praising God and prophesying.

Had it not been Zechariah's house, it would have been

unthinkable. No one would leave their work, much less their dinner, to run to witness a strange girl—a Galilean no less!—show such disrespect for her elders and betters by daring to proclaim God's plan! What was Zechariah thinking, to let her go on like this? Oh yes, they all knew that Israel had had women prophets. Miriam, Hannah, Deborah, all women of God, certainly. But they were, well, astonishing women! Matrons, warriors, leaders among women and men. And they were all related to men who defined their status. Miriam, prophetess and sister to Moses and Aaron! Hannah, mother of Samuel, God's own priest and anointer of kings! Deborah, choice of God to be Israel's wise and courageous judge. These women, along with Sarah and Rebecca, Leah and Rachel, Esther and Ruth, Judith and Susanna—they were all known to God and to them.

But this slender girl before them, who was she? What had she done to make anyone believe she should be standing there announcing God's words? Who was she, other than a distant relation from a village even smaller and less favored than theirs? Who were her parents but poor residents of the outpost called Nazareth? Who was her husband but a carpenter unknown to anyone in Judea?

And yet. They were mesmerized by the slight, swaying figure beside Zechariah. Once there, they couldn't have walked away if they'd wanted to. This girl, no older than some of their daughters—their *obedient* daughters already quietly betrothed or married with firstborns and who wouldn't dream of making spectacles of themselves like this one—seemed to draw and hold their attention despite themselves. What was it about her?

They wondered. Her dark, luminous eyes held theirs even when they wanted to look away. Her strong, clear voice filled their ears and then their minds, and her words, though familiar to all who knew the holy writings, were somehow different coming from her. Her very demeanor, though she appeared bedraggled and travel-worn, emanated joy and energy as they imagined only an angel might. None of them felt able to look away.

Zechariah saw their fascination, their curiosity, and no matter how they tried to hide it, their hope. And he laughed soundlessly.

For Mary and her Judean Family

Zechariah knew why they couldn't look away, couldn't even move until Mary had finished her canticle. He and Elizabeth both understood what their bewildered, anxious neighbors could only begin to sense. They were hearing the fulfillment of God's promise. They were hearing not just the promise repeated, but the promise made real. *They don't comprehend it,* Zechariah thought, *but they feel it. In the depths of their souls, through the journey of millennia, in the bones of their ancestors, they feel Mary's words.*

They still would not allow themselves to believe—he could see that in their eyes, at least in the eyes of the men. A few of the younger women, unfettered by the men's bias against hearing God's words from a girl's mouth, seemed to grasp what Mary was saying. They moved closer to her, their eyes shining. Elizabeth noticed one of them, a girl not much older than Mary who was thought to be ill-treated by her older, relatively wealthy husband, reach out as if to touch Mary's hand. Her husband was a proud man who thought he knew all there was to know about Scripture, about God, about life. He was constantly arguing with Zechariah and the other elders, believing that his money and his status made him an expert in everything. He had taken great relish in Zechariah's enforced silence, encouraging the whispers about the cause of it. *Yes*, thought Elizabeth as she watched his child-bride's wan and thin face come alive, *yes, raise up your eyes, my poor daughter; this is for you, these words are for you.*

It might have been easier for them to forget the promise and protection of the Almighty, but they hadn't. Though none of them could remember a time when Israel was not beleaguered and oppressed, when they were not forced to serve pagans and Gentiles, throughout all of it, they had remembered the Lord. They had believed, sometimes by just a thread of hope, that he would not forget them. Despite the betrayal of some of their leaders, even some of the priests and Pharisees, they had clung to the hope of God's mercy, believing that he would turn and see their atonements, their humility, their abject need. Had not their very own prophets predicted that the day would come when God would restore them to his favor, destroy their arrogant oppressors, and reveal them to the world once again as his very own? Were not the songs of David and the Korahites filled with reminders of God's power? "They shall sing of the ways of the Lord, for great is the glory of the Lord. For though the Lord is high, he regards the lowly; but the haughty he perceives from far away" (Psalm 138:5–6).

The words passed through Zechariah's mind and would have moved over his tongue had not God silenced him for his own foolish doubt. He gazed helplessly from his wife and the boy she carried, to Mary whose Son was still safely hidden within her, to his neighbors, some of them curious, others scandalized, a few thrilled. If only he could tell them what was happening to them!

Then he and Elizabeth watched with the villagers as Mary stretched out her arm and entwined her fingers with those of the frightened young wife.

And Mary said, "He has shown strength with his arm; he has scattered the proud in the thoughts of their hearts."

For the World

There is no indication that the rest of the world so much as paused while Mary spoke to a few astonished Hebrews in Judea. The proud and wise and crafty of the world might have wasted a moment laughing scornfully if they knew a girl from Nazareth was prophesying to a handful of powerless villagers in the south. But they didn't know, and so Caesar Augustus did not hesitate while practicing his latest oration. It is not written that the tetrarch Herod choked a little on the wine he'd commissioned from the finest grapes of a vineyard he'd stolen from its Jewish tenants. Or that his young son and heir watched greedily while the gluttonous Herod sputtered and gurgled, wondering when he would sit on his father's throne. Nor is there any record of Pontius Pilate's parents having a moment's errant or disturbing doubt about the plan they were making for their ambitious young son.

Even as Mary spoke, was wise Melchior tossing away his meticulously crafted maps in frustration, and simply looking to the sky? Was brilliant Balthasar abandoning his search in the sacred texts for the precise identity of the One they sought, and surrendering to his hopes? Was Gaspar surprised to find himself suddenly unconcerned about which of them had brought the more valuable gift as he drove his camel onward?

They were all powerful, all wise in the ways of the world, all proud, all rulers of their lands. None of them could know the anguish of being a Jew in Palestine or the wider world. None of them had experienced hunger, humiliation, sorrow, or loss. None of them understood what it was to be hunted and hated simply because they belonged to God. None of them knew what it was to feel rejected and abandoned because they had forgotten God. None of them could know what it was to be Job, the man who had come to symbolize for the Jews—and would come to symbolize for all who know Scripture—the tragedy and triumph of belonging to God "who frustrates the devices of the crafty, so that their hands achieve no success. He takes the wise in their own craftiness; and the schemes of the wily are brought to a quick end" (Job 5:12–13).

There were others in the world at that moment who did know what Mary spoke of, if not perfectly, than at least through their own experience. Simeon and Anna, who roamed the temple in Jerusalem a few miles from where Mary spoke, had waited decades for her words and for the child she would show them in a few short months; they would have known. Impoverished shepherds who put their bodies between their sheep and all human and wild predators not far from where Mary stood—they would have known. The slaves building Herod's palaces and serving Roman senators and laboring in the bowels of Pharaoh's ships—they would have known. But they were not kings and queens or generals and bloody warriors. They were not wealthy merchants or statesmen who heaped up riches that had been carried upon the broken and bleeding backs of servants. They were not scholars and astronomers who sought answers in the universe's elements rather than in its Creator.

And Mary said, "He has shown strength with his arm; he has scattered the proud in the thoughts of their hearts."

For Us

We cannot afford to take comfort in thinking that Mary's *Magnificat*, a summary of all God had been to the Jews and would be to the rest of us, was meant as an admonishment only to the Caesars, Herods, Pilates, Pharisees, Pharaohs, Magi, merchants, warriors, and senators of her day. Nor should we fear that it was meant to comfort only the shepherds, slaves, workers, and all the humbly faithful and oppressed of the world two millennia past.

The *Magnificat* is both an admonition and a comfort for all of us today, and whether we take it as an admonition or a comfort depends upon us. For many of us, it is probably a lot of both. This verse particularly applies to we who have come so far from the quiet girl of Nazareth and her Son. Because make no mistake, Mary's *Magnificat* is nothing more or less than Jesus' opening statement, made by his mother. He will go on to inculcate humility almost every time he acts and speaks in the gospels.

He selects uneducated tradesmen and sinners as apostles. He blesses and delights in children and warns repeatedly that we must be like them to enter the kingdom of God; one of the few times Jesus expresses anger toward the apostles is when they try to keep children from him. He is impressed with seemingly powerless women like the widow contributing her last coins, the Canaanite woman who embraces humiliation to seek a cure for her child, the widow of Nain who has lost son and husband, the Samaritan woman who is an outcast for her sexual and marital history, the hemorrhaging woman who cringes at his feet in hopeful abeyance.

Later both Peter and Paul will emphasize Jesus' call to humility, and Paul will present himself, sometimes at great length, as an example. But perhaps Peter, who was repeatedly humbled by Jesus for three entire years, offers the most poignant statement on humility when he instructs the early Christians: "And all of you must clothe yourselves with humility in your dealings with one another, for 'God opposes the proud but gives grace to the humble.' Humble yourselves, therefore, under the mighty hand of God" (1 Peter 5:5–6). Peter had learned that lesson—at the end in the hardest possible way—and knew how important it was to those who would follow Christ.

Just as Jesus counseled humility, always welcoming the simple- and single-minded, he cautioned against arrogance and the world's wisdom, openly mocking the wise, proud, and powerful. From his not-so-gentle teasing of the Scripture scholar Nicodemus, to naming Herod a fox, to furiously ejecting the money changers and merchants from the temple, to excoriating the Pharisees, scribes, and lawyers, Jesus was far from reticent in making it clear that those who present power, wealth, and wisdom as evidence of their closeness to God are at great risk of losing their way to him altogether.

We can't truly know at what point Jesus fully comprehended his purpose or what the Father would demand of him. But in his love, practice, and promotion of humility, we do know that he was his mother's Son.

And Mary said, "He has shown strength with his arm; he has scattered the proud in the thoughts of their hearts."

Praying and Discussing the *Magnificat* Today

PRAYER

Mary, how do I become humble? How do I become one who can be consoled by your words, rather than fear them? I live in one of the most powerful and wealthy countries of the world. I am never hungry out of necessity, never thirsty for lack of water, never without decent clothes. I am not a slave, not even a servant, and I am almost always paid something for my work. Relative to the rest of the world, I can hardly call myself oppressed or downtrodden. And yet, I am a slave to sin, a servant of my appetites and perceived needs. I am oppressed by personal and global fears, ashamed of my failings, humiliated by the failings of my nation. I am hungry for God, thirsty for God's word, unclothed in my naked pride. Mary, just as your Son saved Nicodemus from his so-called wisdom, Peter from his foolish pride, Paul from his murderous arrogance, help me to be humbled in my weakness and humanity. Amen.

QUESTIONS

1. To whom do you think Mary was referring in this verse when she speaks of God scattering the thoughts of the proud? Do you think she was simply speaking in the Holy Spirit about the proud of all ages past and to come? Or might she have been referring to specific individuals or groups at the time? To whom do you think her listeners thought she was referring?

2. Do you consider yourself humble? In what way or ways? Is it possible to be both wise and foolish? Proud and humble? What are you most proud of about yourself? Do you consider those things that make you proud as gifts from God or as skills/traits/work you've developed mostly on your own?

SEVEN

The Lowly Lifted

And Mary said, "He has brought down the powerful
from their thrones, and lifted up the lowly." LUKE 1:52

SETTING THE SCENE

E lizabeth is startled to see that a number of children have crept up to the edge of the yard, one or two following their parents, but some out of curiosity. It is not often that a crowd gathers in front of a household in the middle of an afternoon when there is no holiday meal or celebration. She knows that the older children are happy to take any opportunity to shirk their chores, but there is something in Mary's voice and demeanor that attracts them for reasons they cannot name. One little girl, whom Elizabeth recognizes as her closest neighbor's granddaughter, cannot take her eyes off Mary. Elizabeth laughs softly as the girl boldly toddles right up and plops herself down at Mary's feet. Two others, a boy and girl who are just as small, follow, and their parents make no attempt to stop them. The parents, Elizabeth realizes, are just as fascinated as the children.

Elizabeth studies the children. For so many years she

has watched children, children who are now adults, children who are now parents themselves, with such longing! If only she could have had one—just one, even a girl, if that was God's will! She did not yearn for a child simply to eradicate her shame and fulfill her duty as a wife and a woman. She yearned in her very bones and organs! Her arms ached to hold an infant and then a young child. Her mind played cruel tricks on her, showing her scene after scene of imaginary children as if to punish her for not giving it one of her own to occupy itself with. Her hands and fingers worked constantly, making small clothes for village little ones and cooking delicacies for those who fussed at their own mother's breasts or cooking.

And here, now, when it should be too late, when the dreams had died, children flock to her home even as she carries her own in her womb. It is as if she has become mother to all of them! But she knows they have not come for her. Mary, both child and mother, is the one they have come for. And Elizabeth, suddenly tired and still a little afraid, is glad of this. Yet what can these children understand of Mary's words? What do they make of this stranger at the edge of their village?

Unexpected tears burn Elizabeth's eyes, and she shades her face with one hand, her other pressed firmly on her belly. She has the sharp and painful sense that her John will never be as easy and happy as these little ones. She cannot see, in her hopeful mind's eye, her little boy finding pure joy and play in the company of other children. She realizes as she listens to the tiny girl chattering at Mary's feet that the day has become like a festival. But she can't help fearing what the rest are celebrating.

Zechariah touches her hand where it lies on her stomach. She glances quickly at him and then away. Though he cannot speak, they have a language between them that has grown over their years together, and he gently pulls her hand away from her face and looks deeply into her brimming eyes. The delight he has taken in Mary is tempered by what he sees in his wife's face and what he is beginning to feel in his own heart.

Some pride has crept, inevitably, into his pleasure at Mary's presence and in her words. Though ecstatic and overwhelmed with awe at the meaning of Mary and her song, he has not been able to help himself from feeling at least somewhat vindicated. After all, God has kept him silent for so long! Him, a man who loves to speak, to proclaim God, to debate his holy words and law—for him to have been made mute for doubting the angel's words stung so deeply that it had robbed him of some of the joy of God's promise coming to pass in Elizabeth's pregnancy. To be truthful with himself, finally, he has felt humiliated before his neighbors and the other villagers, as much because of their pity as their whisperings. For all the years that he had been God's priest and had spoken of God's words, when he'd been given the most important message of all, the most important message ever, he'd squandered the opportunity to speak it.

For Mary and her Judean Family

So when Mary had come—come to *him*, to *his* wife, to *their* home—bearing her still secret child and speaking her sacred words, well! Zechariah felt it was a gift from the Almighty, a sign that he was still favored and forgiven and, in the fullness of time, would be given his voice back. And,

God forgive him, he had felt elevated once again before his people, restored to his rightful place of authority as a priest and elder.

But now, watching the children gather in the yard to hear and be close to Mary, and seeing the pain of premonition in Elizabeth's eyes, the gold and silver that had been pride rising in his heart has become like iron. The weight of it was sinking, coming to rest in what felt like the very center of his being, solid and irrefutable, now a part of him. And somehow Zechariah knows that despite his delight at God fulfilling his covenant, the iron will remain within him for the rest of his life. God forbid that it would be longer than that of his son's, or Mary's Son's.

Zechariah takes Elizabeth's hand, the one she'd raised to hide her eyes as if from the blazing sun, and holds it.

Mary at this moment was standing at the center of God's timeline. She may not have known it. And for all that Zechariah and Elizabeth knew about God's promise of a Messiah to redeem Israel, they probably didn't fully realize it either. Those who heard Mary in that Judean village, if they understood at all, would have understood her to be announcing the coming of a time of favor for Israel. They would have understood her words to be rooted in prophets and prophecies of the past, from Hannah and Moses to Isaiah and Jeremiah. They would have heard her announcing a completion, a fulfillment, the best ending ever for Israel! Even those who knew every word of the Hebrew Scriptures at the time, and not many villagers probably did, could not have imagined that she was also proclaiming a beginning, indeed, the best beginning ever for the rest of God's people.

And the *Magnificat*, in its similarity to Hannah's song of praise and other prayers, particularly those of biblical women, makes it clear who God's people are. God's people are not the high and mighty, the lords and ladies, the power-hungry. They are not those who sit on thrones or wear diadems.

Though God is merciful, he is not to be fooled by the trappings and machinations of power. Indeed, it is quite the opposite: God is with the poor and broken. In this verse of the *Magnificat*, the word *lowly* no longer refers to God's individual servants like Hannah and Mary, but to the lowly of the world now and to come. "The Lord is a God of knowledge, and by him actions are weighed. The bows of the mighty are broken, but the feeble gird on strength" (1 Samuel 2:3–4). God's people are the lowly, those most in need of his attention and mercy. They are the ones who have felt the cruelty of kings, the selfishness of rulers, the arrogance of governors. They are the ones who have been waiting, silent and suffering, for God to rescue them.

They are the ones in Judean hill villages who gather eagerly, despite their traditions and suspicions, to hear the words of a poor girl from the alien north.

And Mary said, "He has brought down the powerful from their thrones, and lifted up the lowly."

FOR THE WORLD

Did the rulers of those days have even the slightest idea of what was really going in Nazareth and Judea, in Bethlehem and Jerusalem? Of course, they couldn't have known this young girl was proclaiming their downfall to a scraggly group of her relative's neighbors. And if they had, they might not even have bothered to imprison, kill, or crucify her as they had other rebels. They might have thought her unworthy of the effort.

But did they have any concept of how God was using them to move history? Did any of the Caesars understand that by oppressing the Jews and their religious traditions, God was leading the Roman rulers to set the stage for the historical and spiritual Messiah? Did Augustus know that by proclaiming a census, he would ensure that a Son of Nazareth would instead be born in Bethlehem, thus fulfilling God's Scripture? Could Herod have understood that by driving the Holy Family from Bethlehem with the order to slaughter all male toddlers, he was offering the best camouflage possible to Jesus by forcing the young family into Egypt and then to Nazareth, two places that few would have thought the Messiah to come from? Did the Roman governors of Palestine, even before Pilate, realize that by placing political appointees among the high priests and Pharisees, they were making it that much easier for the Jewish people to turn *away* from their nominal leaders and *toward* Jesus?

The rulers of the world had no clue that God was driving them because they had no concept of the omniscient God. In their immense hubris, they could not even imagine how God's infinite power would render their puny human ambitions useless. Even the Pharisees and leaders, enjoying the favor of the Roman overlords, failed to heed what the psalmist had long since comprehended: "For not from the east or from the west or from wilderness comes lifting up; but it is God who executes judgment, putting down one thing and lifting up another" (Psalm 75:6–7).

But are today's world leaders, with all the advantages of

religious knowledge, technology, and global communication, any better? Do our presidents and kings, prime ministers and shahs and premiers, our popes and rabbis and imams and yogis and gurus, our chief executive officers and corporate boards and trustees and academics, understand that all the knowledge and control they think they have amassed is like a pebble in the sea of God's power?

As I write this, Israel and Hamas are savaging each other in Gaza, the Ukraine is engaged in what amounts to a civil war that has brought the US and Russia to the brink of a dangerous conflict, Islamic extremists are threatening to slaughter Christians in a village within their newly declared caliphate borders, Americans are arguing over immigration while tens of thousands of children languish at the US-Mexican border—some to be deported back to places where they will be raped and enslaved—and the so-called Arab Spring has become a brutal winter where not even the smallest of green shoots can survive.

It appears that the answer is no.

And Mary said, "He has brought down the powerful from their thrones, and lifted up the lowly."

For Us

And so, it is up to us to remember who God is and to whom we belong. It is so easy to forget! We put so much stock in the leaders and rulers of the world, both secular and religious, across all political systems and religious traditions. We elect them, either directly or indirectly; we invest in them; we want to trust them; we watch what they eat and wear, how and where they live; we are avid for them to be what we want them to be. Most of all, we so want to believe that God is with them that we sometimes forget that it is they—and we—who must prove ready and willing to be with God.

The fact is that God was with the lowly when Mary spoke, and God is with the lowly now. Are we ready and willing to count ourselves among the lowly? Do we even know how?

Over thirty years after Mary's words, her Son would echo them, almost precisely, in the Beatitudes, confirming God's announcement through her *Magnificat*, and speaking not only to a few perplexed and anxious Judeans but to all humankind. "When Jesus saw the crowds, he went up the mountain…and taught them, saying: 'Blessed are the poor in spirit, for theirs is the kingdom of heaven. Blessed are those who mourn, for they will be comforted. Blessed are the meek, for they will inherit the earth'" (Matthew 5:1–5).

What joy his listeners must have felt! What unexpected, unlikely, seemingly impossible (for nothing is impossible with God) delight they must have felt! Who had spoken such comfort to them before Jesus? Who had said such words—revolutionary words!—to so many at one time? Who had so precisely named their very state of apparent wretchedness, and then renamed it blessed?

And for us, too, there is hope in the instructive nature of Jesus' blessings. Do we want to be blessed? Then we must be humble, poor in spirit. Then we should mourn our losses and the losses of every person in the world. Then we should be meek, avoiding any opportunity to hurt or contend with or triumph over another. Then we should weep for the many who feel the loss of God, and speak peace to those

who hate peace, and allow ourselves to go hungry so that
we can better appreciate how so many of God's people live.

It is simple for us to be lowly. It's just not easy.

And Mary said, "He has brought down the powerful
from their thrones, and lifted up the lowly."

Praying and Discussing the *Magnificat* Today

PRAYER

*Mary, I wonder if I have ever felt lowly, truly lowly, in the
way you described yourself and in the way Jesus blessed the
crowds? In my heart, it is not easy for me to consider lowliness a good thing, and yet I know your words and Jesus'
words and the words of the gospels. I know God is with
the lowly of this world, and so I long to be what I fear to
be! Mary, help me! Teach me that lowliness requires me to
depend upon God in a way that will make me blessed and
bring me blessings. Help me to understand that worldly
power is always temporary and often corrupt. Show me to
use what "power" or influence or wealth I have in a "lowly"
manner so that I may do only God's will with God's gifts to
me. Let those who suffer in this world always be in my heart
and mind and prayers. Give me the kind of empathy that
will lead me to live the life God wishes me to live. Amen.*

QUESTIONS

1. What is your definition of lowly? What is your
    definition of power? When you consider the
    Magnificat and the Beatitudes, are your definitions
    changed in any way?

2. How would you describe yourself on the continuum of lowliness and power? Is it possible to be both lowly and powerful? If you believe it is, how is it possible? Can you name anyone who is both?

EIGHT

The Hungry Filled

*And Mary said, "He has filled the hungry with good things,
and sent the rich away empty."* LUKE 1:53

SETTING THE SCENE

The pressure of Zechariah's hand on hers changes
ever so slightly, and Elizabeth glances swiftly
at her husband. Without needing to meet her
eyes, he inclines his head almost imperceptibly
toward four newcomers to the group gathering in front
of their dwelling. Instantly she understands. This is the
first family that has come together to hear Mary, but that,
Elizabeth knows, is not the only thing that has caught
Zechariah's attention. This young couple with the little
girl clinging to her mother's skirts and the boy, not yet a
year old, held in his father's arms, are new not just to this
group, but to the village.

They'd arrived the year before, having made the long
trek from Galilee, though not from Nazareth. They'd lived
in a town near Mary's, but they did not speak of their
home other than to say that they'd been unable to pay
Herod's latest tax, added to the already onerous Roman

levy, and so had lost their land. When Zechariah, shortly before Gabriel had taken his voice, had gone to greet them, they had been vague about why they'd settled in the Judean hills, only saying the obvious: they needed work. They had taken a tenancy in a room rented by the owner of the vineyard where they worked.

"What little money they make, he takes in rent," Zechariah had told Elizabeth at the time, but not because the man had complained. Neither the husband nor the wife was inclined to speak much, and the rest of the villagers kept mostly away from them, both granting their evident wish for privacy and sparing themselves any great effort to welcome the northerners. Zechariah, on the other hand, went out of his way to include the young family, but to no avail. Ignoring Zechariah's overtures, the man never joined in debates about Scripture or the angry discussions about Rome, despite having lost everything to the occupiers.

Not long after Zechariah's voice was taken, the man had given him a searching, sympathetic look; that night, with a wry expression on his face, Zechariah handed Elizabeth a tablet with a few words written on it: "he likes me better when I cannot speak to him." Elizabeth had laughed, but she herself was having no great success with the wife. The young woman shyly resisted all attempts by Elizabeth and a few of the elder women to talk about her children or the family she must have left behind. Noticing that both children and parents were thin and sallow-skinned despite working all day in the sun, Zechariah and Elizabeth had tried to offer food or at least share their more abundant Sabbath meals, but the man gruffly resisted all such efforts, making his disdain of charity clear.

Now here they were, standing apart from their neighbors, watching Mary closely. Elizabeth, not needing the tablet to know her husband's thoughts, went into the house to bring out the bread she'd baked that morning. Her eyes fell upon the goat milk curds and olives she'd been curing. There was probably not enough for everyone, but...why not? Elizabeth thought. Mary must be hungry after her journey, and perhaps her neighbors from Galilee could be persuaded to join her. Just this once.

For Mary and her Judean Family

By this time in Israel's history, much of the land of milk and honey had become the land of toil and scarcity. Except for a short period under the Maccabees, Israelites and Judeans had not freely owned the land they occupied and sowed for centuries. Some of the Jews who had been dispersed had never returned to Palestine even when free to do so. Having achieved a level of success while in exile, those of the diaspora had preferred to practice their trades and professions in the countries where they had been taken even when they were free to return to Israel. Most of those who had returned, especially those in the north, Galilee and Nazareth, were subsistence farmers, barely growing enough to feed themselves and their families.

Even those fortunate and wealthy enough to own or plant fertile land in Israel and Judea had to give up the lion's share of what they reaped to whatever nation ruled over them; at this time, it was Rome. But Herod and his small empire were not lax about robbing the people of their hard-earned money. The Herodians in the region had undertaken to construct not only palaces and elaborate homes for themselves, but also infrastructure throughout the land. The cost was enormous, and Rome was certainly not going to help. The price for the Herodian legacy of construction fell most heavily on the Jewish and Samaritan peasants and shepherds. Many of these, and probably some among those listening to Mary, quite literally had to choose between paying taxes to Herod and Ceasar or going to bed hungry.

Jewish Scripture, often through prophets like Jeremiah, suggested that God's people had lost his protection by not obeying and worshiping only him; thus, they would be scattered and their land taken by infidels and pagans. Isaiah and other prophets had repeated the promise of God's Messiah, the One who would come and restore the land and God's favor to his people. Those listening to Mary would have been very familiar with these tenets of their tradition.

In Psalm 107, entitled Thanksgiving for Deliverance from Many Troubles, the psalmist repeats a pattern of naming the sins and failings of God's people, only to reveal God's constant readiness to deliver them from their own sins. "Let the redeemed of the Lord say so, those he redeemed from trouble and gathered in from the lands, from the east and from the west, from the north and from the south. Some wandered in desert wastes, finding no way to an inhabited town; hungry and thirsty, their soul fainted within them. Then they cried to the Lord in their trouble, and he delivered them from their distress. For he satisfies the thirsty, and the hungry he fills with good things" (Psalm 107:2–6, 9).

The psalm continues in this vein, noting God's willingness to lead his people back to him, back to places where he has made food and water abundant, to a place newly flowing with milk and honey. The people of Mary's time were hungry not just for the chance to eat of their own crops and drink fresh water and wine from lands they'd struggled to irrigate; they also hungered for a return to God's favor, to be filled with the good things that come with God's forgiveness and love. These things, they believed, would be brought by God's Messiah.

And Mary said, "He has filled the hungry with good things, and sent the rich away empty."

FOR THE WORLD

The useless idols of the rest of the world, those false forms worshiped by the Greeks and Druids and Romans and Egyptians and Persians, were believed to show favor almost exclusively to the rich and powerful. In other words, those who sacrificed most lavishly to them were those expected to reap the greatest benefit from their nonexistent benevolence. Some of the wealthiest rulers even kept temples on or in their own property to their favorite idol, thus associating themselves, their ambitions, and their success with one particular false deity. The logic went something like this: if someone was wealthy and powerful, then obviously it must be because Zeus or Aphrodite or Isis or Mars favored that person. The expectation that one of these mythological idols would turn on its rich patron and instead raise up the masses of poor who suffered under the whims of the ruling class was exceedingly unlikely.

Of course, these pagan traditions made it easy for the rest of the world to ignore God and his people. They believed that if God truly loved the Hebrews, they would all be rich and successful, not enslaved and oppressed. Rome knew well that those few Semitic people who held power in Palestine—like Herod and some of the Pharisees and chief priests—did so at Caesar's pleasure. Surely the rest of the world, they reasoned, had nothing to fear from a God who had seemingly abandoned his people. The pagan religious worldview made it all but impossible for the people or their leaders to understand God, much less his people.

But the massive world that surrounded Palestine and considered it little more than an annoying source of revenue was about to learn about the one, true God. The God of the people they'd despised and abused did not favor the rich and the strong. He did not bestow good gifts upon the arrogant and mighty. He did not heap riches upon those who already had too much for their own good. He did not gaze benevolently upon those who enslaved the poor and laid heavy burdens on the desolate.

And the rest of the world was about to hear his voice.

And Mary said, "He has filled the hungry with good things, and sent the rich away empty."

FOR US

Contrasting with Mathew's version discussed earlier, in Luke's Beatitudes Jesus offers a chilling counterpart to his blessings: the woes. As with Mary uttering the *Magnificat*, Jesus is speaking primarily to people who hunger for everything: food, dignity, independence, and an end to their servitude and Roman-Herodian oppression. After encouraging the crowd with the blessings, Jesus then speaks words of warning to those who would keep the masses hungry and oppressed: "Woe to you who are rich, for you have received your consolation. Woe to you who are full now, for you will be hungry" (Luke 6:24–25). The message of both Jesus and Mary is the same in at least one essential way: God is about to flip the world onto its ear, and everyone—not just the poor and disenfranchised—had better pay attention.

It is important for us to remember that, aside from the words of a few Jewish prophets, before Jesus there was no concept of a religion that favored the destitute and the powerless. This is hard for us, as products of Jesus' teachings, as Christians, to understand. We have been raised to believe, though not always to act upon the belief, that the poor are the focus of God's attention and mercy. But this idea had revolutionary implications at the time of Mary and Jesus. While Judaism incorporated and even inculcated compassion for the poor, it generally focused on the poor of the Israelites. Now, in this verse and in much of the *Magnificat*, we have Mary using familiar language to announce what would become, under Jesus' guidance, an unfamiliar concept: God is not just for the Jews, or the poor among the Jews, but for the poor and oppressed throughout the world.

That was true for the world then and the world to come—in other words, for our world. The challenge for each of us is to understand in what ways we are among the rich in this age—and even the poor in America are better off than much of the rest of the world—and in what ways we are among the poor. While many of us never need to go to bed hungry, some of us are famished for God's word, for consolation, for mercy, for healing, for forgiveness, for refuge, for strength, for encouragement, for God's help. In those ways we are very much like those who heard Mary's words and Jesus' sermon. We are spiritually impoverished and starving, in desperate need of God's intervention in our lives.

Thus, where we are rich, we need to admit it and strive to be generous and avoid relying on riches instead of on God; and where we are poor, we must also acknowledge our poverty and seek God's presence zealously. When we find ourselves hungering more deeply for God than for rich food and money, we will know we are moving in the right direction.

And Mary said, "He has filled the hungry with good things, and sent the rich away empty."

Praying and Discussing the *Magnificat* Today

Prayer

Mary, I wonder how often you were hungry as a child, a woman, and especially during your pregnancy. You had to learn, literally, to be filled with God, who then satisfied all your hungers. Teach me, Blessed Mother, to rely on God to fill me in my spiritual and emotional poverty with good things. Help me to reject the power of wealth and over-indulgence in rich food to satisfy me so that I may be more ready to accept the power of God. Help me to remember that everything I think of as mine, including every morsel of food, is actually provided to me by God and is neither earned nor gotten by me. Show me that the best way to fill my emptiness is with spiritual food and with the Body and Blood of your Son, our Lord, Jesus Christ. Amen.

Questions

1. How well do you tolerate physical hunger? Do you ever deliberately allow yourself to feel hungry so that you can experience that feeling? Do you think of food as a gift from God? Do you ever feel compelled to share food with those who have less than you?

2. If you were to ask God to, as Mary says, "fill you with good things," what good things would you be thinking of?

NINE

His Servant Helped

And Mary said, "He has helped his servant Israel,
in remembrance of his mercy." LUKE 1:54

SETTING THE SCENE

There were by now enough villagers to fill Zechariah's yard and spill into the path in front of the house. Some of the youngest had settled down on the ground, their eyes never leaving Mary's face. As Elizabeth brought out the food she could gather from her own kitchen, a few of her nearest neighbors disappeared inside their own homes and returned with whatever they could spare. One brought wine; another pressed olive oil for the bread. Some ate, and others didn't, but Zechariah could see that no one who might want or need food was going without. At first, Elizabeth had been dismayed when the proud father of the new family that had come from Galilee shook his head gruffly at her offer of bread and olives. Turning his face from Elizabeth, he even moved to pull back the hands of his little girl, when she reached eagerly for the bread. His wife had looked away, but

Elizabeth saw the flush, the tears in her eyes, the battle waged within her between her child's hunger and her husband's pride.

Anger had flared in Elizabeth, and she might have chastised the man herself, but at that moment, Mary paused and studied the family. She came and gently took the food from Elizabeth and gave it to the children, as if the father had not just rejected the gift. When Mary looked into the man's eyes, his face fell and his shoulders sloped downward helplessly. She reached her hand out to him, but he shrunk from her touch, ashamed. She did not move, waiting, as though trying to tame a wild creature, until finally he looked up. She did nothing more than incline her head slightly toward him, looking up at him with a small, quizzical smile. Then she took the basket of bread from Elizabeth and gave it to the man, gesturing that he was to pass it out among the others. This is the work Mary gave him to do as his children ate and his wife gazed at her with silent gratitude. He gave bread to his neighbors, greeting some of them for the first time since arriving in Judea with his family.

For Mary and her Judean Family

Watching Mary intervene with the Galilean family as she wordlessly drew them into the heart of the village, Zechariah thought to himself, *She has done more in this moment than I or Elizabeth or any other has done to make them welcome since they came here. What is it in her that allows her to make such a thing possible? How can she draw people together who have been little more than strangers?* Then, seeing the man accept some of the wine for himself with an awkward nod of thanks, Zechariah understood: *Mary is merciful!*

She is just a girl, and yet she has a quality of mercy that he has not seen except in very old and very kind people. Zechariah tried to remember the other times, just a few occasions over the years, when he had seen Mary. Though he had been married to Elizabeth for decades now, Mary was only thirteen or fourteen, and they had not celebrated many festivals or even weddings with the family from Nazareth. He had only a vague image of her parents, Anna and Joachim. He knew that Mary was born late to them, though not as late as John would be born to him and Elizabeth. Zechariah searched his mind for memories of those few gatherings, memories of Mary, but all he could find were fragments.

Fragments like a softly chattering, pretty toddler sitting on Joachim's knee, feeding him bits of honeyed cake that most children would have greedily stuffed in their own mouths. A quiet, smiling young child watching her mother and Elizabeth as they wove or milled grain for bread and talked. A silent, watchful girl, drinking in every word he, Joachim, and the other men exchanged about the hubris of Rome, the greed of the Herodians, and the law of Moses. When Elizabeth had told him some months ago that Mary had been betrothed, he thought little of it except to marvel at the passing of time that had made that charming baby into a girl ready for marriage.

And now she was here, the definition of mercy, carrying God's very incarnation of mercy. The words of a psalm passed through Zechariah's mind, and he dearly wished they could have passed over his still silent lips: "He has remembered his steadfast love and faithfulness to the house of Israel. All the ends of the earth have seen the victory of God. For he is coming to judge the earth. He will judge the world with righteousness and the people with equity" (Psalm 98:3, 9). Were it not for the heat of the sun, the presence of his neighbors, the strong hand of his wife, now back at his side, grasping his, Zechariah might well have thought he was experiencing another vision. *Is the whole thing a dream?* he wondered wildly. Would he wake to find that he had never served in the temple, or seen Gabriel, or been struck dumb because of his doubt, or fathered the child in Elizabeth's womb? Would he wake to find his poor wife still barren and Mary nothing but a distant memory from a long-ago family gathering? If this was not a dream, how could it be happening? To him? Why had God picked this time, his family, to manifest a promise made so many generations ago when his people were still freshly in love with God and still deeply fearful of him?

Zechariah began to tremble, overwhelmed by these thoughts, and though Elizabeth's grip on his hand grew tighter, he felt overwhelmed with fear. Surely this must all be a dream, he thought, for how am I worthy of this unspeakable gift, this impossible burden? Mary turned from the Galilean family and looked searchingly at Zechariah. Then she smiled.

And Mary said, "He has helped his servant Israel, in remembrance of his mercy."

For the World

While the *Magnificat*, especially this verse, resounds with many similar fragments from a variety of psalms, Mary's reference to Zechariah's psalm (Psalm 98, above) is as much an immediate prophecy as it is a summation of history; remember, Mary carries God coming to judge the earth. She knows this. Gabriel has told her that her Son is not only the promised Messiah but also that "the Lord God will give him the throne of his ancestor David. He will reign over the house of Jacob forever, and of his kingdom there will be no end" (Luke 1:32–33). While Mary may not fully comprehend how God intends to judge the world through her Son, she surely understands that the One to reign over the house of Jacob forever will certainly be charged with the duty of judging his people. And as the mother of that child, forming in her even as she speaks, she must have a sense that if God intended to send a warrior Messiah, he would probably not have selected a kind, gentle girl from Nazareth to be his mother.

In spite of Mary's humility and the *Magnificat*'s implicit instruction that God favors the humble, there is something distinctly triumphant in its tenor, particularly in these last verses. It is almost as if the pure, heretofore quiet virgin from the north cannot quite keep the exultation out of her proclamation. Whatever the future will bring, she is living proof that, as her Son will later declare, salvation is from the Jews, and God's promise must first be fulfilled through them. "But you, Israel, my servant, Jacob, whom I have chosen, the offspring of Abraham, my friend; you whom I took from the ends of the earth, and called from its farthest corners, saying to you, 'You are my servant, I have chosen you and not cast you off'; do not fear, for I am with you, do not be afraid, for I am your God" (Isaiah 41:8–10). Take note, though, that in Isaiah's prophecy, while God's

promise is first made to Jacob, or Israel, he had already
promised Abraham, referred to here as God's friend, that
he would father many nations. Those nations would come
in line for their share of God's promise, too; indeed, Mary
is announcing that their day has come.

The *Magnificat*, then, can be contrasted to the song of
Miriam, sister of Moses, after God destroyed the Egyptians
who defied him by pursuing the Israelites. Miriam's song of
praise and adoration is harsher, more martial, while Mary's
canticle suggests that the Messiah's imminent victory will
be based in God remembering his promise of mercy. The
Messiah's triumph will be founded on God's decision to help
his people, *all* of his people, past, present, and yet to come.

And Mary said, "He has helped his servant Israel, in remembrance of his mercy."

For Us

What does mercy look like? I envision it as a flowing
stream of crystal-clear water, warm and comforting, or
cool and refreshing. I see it as a moving, active force,
meant to emphasize a message or change a situation for
the better. I see it as something that exists to help.

Mercy, especially God's mercy, does not disguise itself.
We need never observe an action and wonder if it is merciful; the action defines itself. If it is a helpful action, it is
based at least in some degree of mercy. Mercy can flow
from empathy, sympathy, pity, forgiveness, kindness, compassion, or even love; but it is none of these things. One
can observe another person or group of people, or perhaps
even a situation, with empathy, sympathy, or pity, but one
cannot really look at someone with mercy; mercy must be

somehow expressed. One can forgive, love, or feel compassion or kindness without feeling compelled to act. Indeed, sometimes these emotions express themselves sternly or with a decided lack of action, as we see in pragmatic advice like "forgive but don't forget."

So all of these important emotions can stand alone as mere feelings or stoic pragmatism, but mercy almost always demands action—and quite often self-sacrificing action. All of these other things are felt; mercy is always shown. Mercy does not frequently demonstrate common sense, nor is it impelled by a survival instinct, the need to protect oneself, or the compulsion to "move on." How often are we counseled to "forgive" or "love" someone who has hurt us, so as to better resolve that situation and move on, for our own sake?

Mercy requires the act of helping. It is often selfless. It does not stop and think about whether its expression is in the best interest of the expresser. It seeks no personal or material gain and seldom achieves one. Mercy is constant; it soothes and heals. Mercy seeks only the good of the one receiving it, not the good of the one giving it.

It can seem that there is not much mercy in our world. It can feel exceedingly difficult to show mercy, to become purely a helper of others. You can feel a bit like a sap, a pushover, a wimp, when you consistently show mercy. It appears to go against everything we are taught about assertiveness, self-esteem, self-love, or cleverness. It is just plain hard.

It must have been hard for Mary to act mercifully toward the world by agreeing to give up her life for God. It must have been hard for God to clothe himself with fleshly

mercy for a world that had given so little to him who de-
served everything. Viewed from these perspectives, maybe
it shouldn't be so hard for us, the recipients of such mercy,
to be merciful.

And Mary said, "He has helped his servant Israel, in remembrance of his mercy."

Praying and Discussing the *Magnificat* Today

PRAYER

*Mary, your entire life was one long and sometimes agoniz-
ing act of mercy. How did you do it? How did you give everything—your life, your marriage, your safety and stability
and well-being, the life of your Son—to show God's mercy to
the world? Merciful mother of Jesus, give me the courage to
show even a fraction of your selfless mercy. Teach me to un-
learn all of those self-protective, self-promoting lessons that
lead me to always put my own interests first. Give me the
strength to transform my feelings of compassion, sympathy,
love, and forgiveness into acts of merciful helping. Help me
to recognize and embrace the opportunities God provides
me to show mercy. Help me to be just a little more like your
Son, and like you. Amen.*

QUESTIONS

1. How do you envision mercy? When was the last time
    you showed mercy? What made you do it? How did
    it feel? Did you act spontaneously? Would you do it
    again?

2. Do you think that human mercy is different from the mercy God shows us? If so, in what way(s)? Or do you think that every act of human mercy is a tiny part of God's mercy at work in us and on earth?

TEN

His Promise Kept

And Mary said, "According to the promise he made to our
ancestors, to Abraham and his descendants forever." LUKE 1:55

SETTING THE SCENE

All the adults among the villagers at Zechariah's house feel that a hundred different thoughts are careening through their minds. They have never experienced anything like this. They have never been so confused and yet so oddly certain. Some are thinking about the chores they left off doing and wondering why they dropped everything to see and hear this girl. Yet they don't want to leave. Some of the wives are wondering what their husbands will say about this, whether their men will think they wasted their time. Yet they are eager to tell them about it. Some of the men wonder why this young girl is allowed to speak of such holy things to a crowd of strangers. Yet they all hope that Zechariah will not stop her. Some are worrying about money and taxes and how to keep their families fed. Yet these are the ones who contribute the most food to the gathering.

What is happening to us? Why are so confounded? Why

are we disturbed and yet elated, frantic and yet filled with peace, terrified and yet overjoyed? What are these feelings that have gripped us so utterly? Are we hearing what we think we are hearing? Is this what we have been waiting for? They are asking themselves these questions silently, and even as they exchange anxious, exultant glances, they have no answers. Zechariah and Elizabeth see this in their faces and in their bodies. The two of them can offer no counsel, for though they understand more fully what is happening than any of their neighbors, this comprehension overwhelms them.

But all of them, particularly the eldest, somewhere in the recesses of their minds, are thinking about their parents, their grandparents, their clan, or their tribe. Elders who have all but forgotten what their parents looked like suddenly have a clear image of them. Younger parents who have only recently lost a parent and who are still grieving have a poignant sense that the lost one is right there beside them. Each of them is abruptly assailed by a memory, perhaps a story told to them as a child, about an ancestor's faith or courage or perseverance. Even the youngest among them who cannot remember the older grandparent or aunt or uncle who died before they could be known finds an image of that person shimmering before their eyes.

There is one thought the villagers all share: what their parents and grandparents, their long-dead ancestors, would have given to see and hear this girl! What would they have made of this? If only they could be consulted! And yet, to every single person in Zechariah's yard, it seems that those who were gone are now, somehow, with them.

FOR MARY AND HER JUDEAN FAMILY

Until now, we've had nothing but words, thought
Elizabeth, and even those have grown dim in the shadow of
our sorrow. It has been so long since our great king David!
It has been so long since God's chosen leader Moses! It has
been so long since Jacob and Isaac and Abraham! Since
then, we have had prophets and travails and loss. Since
then, we have had only the promises to hold onto, and so
many of us let go of even those over the generations. The
farther we have fallen from the Lord, the more we have
been oppressed and pillaged and driven from our home-
land. Egyptians, Persians, Chaldeans, Romans, wave upon
wave of oppression and cruelty and dispersion. How many
of us, over these forty-two generations, have lost sight of
our God, have lost our way, have been more dismayed than
encouraged by the dark words of the prophets? How des-
perately have we staggered to keep the Law, in the face of
betrayal within and enmity without?

But even so, the words of the prophets with their stark
glimmers of hope have mirrored our God's promises to
Abraham, the stern love expressed through Moses, the
unity and humanity demonstrated through his servant
David. Through all this, we've had the words, the words
that moved Abraham to surrender everything—his will
and even his son—to God. "Now the Lord said to Abram,
'Go from your country and your kindred and your father's
house to the land that I will show you. I will make of you
a great nation, and I will bless you, and make your name
great, so that you will be a blessing'" (Genesis 12:1–2).

What courage Abraham must have had! Elizabeth
thought of the son leaping within her womb just a short

while ago. To merely hear the call of God, and leave everything behind! To take a wife and a small group of followers
on a path that would take centuries and still not be com-
plete! How had it been, Elizabeth wondered, for our ancestors? Had Sarah felt Isaac leap in her womb? Did Ismael
leap within the womb of his mother, Hagar? Did Samuel
leap within Hannah's womb? Did Moses' mother feel her
heart leap in fear and joy when she knew the Egyptian
princess had saved her son?

When did the children of Israel, God's chosen children,
stop leaping within the wombs of their mothers? When
did we become a people so oppressed and betrayed by
our leaders, our enemies, ourselves, that we ceased to be
thrilled at the promise of our God? When did we forget
that, under God, new life meant hope, hope for another generation, hope for a fresh chance to experience the
fulfillment of God's promise? Hope that she saw kindling
in the eyes of her neighbors, fixed almost pleadingly on
Mary's face.

And what of Mary's Son? Elizabeth wanted to ask her
young relative. *Does he leap in your womb?*

And Mary said, "According to the promise he made to
our ancestors, to Abraham and his descendants forever."

FOR THE WORLD

In the end Mary, in the *Magnificat*, and Jesus, much later
during his ministry, will say very little that hadn't already
been said and recorded in the Jewish Scriptures. As much
as Jesus will provide radical addendums to the Judaic concepts of justice and compassion, he will build upon the eth-
ical and moral foundation God had already given the Jews.

Just as Mary concisely and beautifully summarizes all of Jewish history in the *Magnificat*, Jesus will strip down the hundreds of Mosaic laws to the teaching of love, telling the disciples that the entire Jewish law can be contained in the commandment to love God and love one another. Jesus is, at once, both God's fulfillment and God's new beginning.

Jesus will take up the thread of history where his mother leaves off in the *Magnificat*—by teaching and embodying the future of God's promise. Yes, the Almighty is fulfilling his promise to his people, but it is a bigger promise than even they understand it to be. It is as though in the disturbing years since the glorious rule of King David, their troubles have eroded the promise in their own hearts, made it shrink along with their hearts and their courage. Mary now, and Jesus later, is revealing that the promise is—and was—profoundly expansive. God chose the Jews first, always knowing that the Jews would lead the rest of the world to him, to his covenant. From this small band of his beloved people, who remained his no matter how they infuriated him, God would draw the entire world to him.

In his letter to the Romans, Paul illustrates this bridge by quoting the prophet Hosea to demonstrate how God opened the promise to include all who would come to believe in his and Mary's Son, Jesus, the Christ: "As indeed he says in Hosea, 'Those who were not my people I will call "my people," and her who was not beloved I will call "beloved."' And in the very place where it was said to them, "You are not my people," there they shall be called children of the Living God" (Romans 9:25–26).

More than any other force, it will be Paul who spreads the good news from the relatively miniscule sphere where

Mary and Jesus lived and taught. Paul, and Peter, will be the first to truly grasp the enormity of God's plan and what it means for the world beyond the Jews and Judea and even all of Palestine. They come to understand that Jesus' "revolution" really began thousands of years earlier and has been freed from all constraints by his life and teachings, death and resurrection.

And Mary said, "According to the promise he made to our ancestors, to Abraham and his descendants forever."

For Us

Where are we in all of this? If, in the *Magnificat*, Mary spoke of the history of God's promise in preparation for Jesus to embody and expand it, are we post-history when it comes to God's covenant? Is there nothing left for us but Scripture, scholarship, and memories?

Quite the contrary. We have inherited both the promise *and* the fulfillment of the promise! And we've been given the Holy Spirit to help us bear up under such a glorious burden. What is our burden? That with knowledge of both the promise and the fulfillment, the New and the Old Testaments, we are the ones who must live out both God's foundation and Jesus' teachings. We are charged with bearing witness to the entire history, the Judeo-Christian law and tradition, which makes us a part of those first called by God.

We are as much the descendants in Mary's last verse of the *Magnificat* as we are those Jesus refers to when he charges the disciples to go out to all nations. We are the ones who came later, the newest generation to be joined with those who belong to God. Though we've come later, we are no less Abraham's descendants, just as we claim Mary as our universal mother: "I will indeed bless you, and I will make your offspring as numerous as the stars of heaven and as the sand that is on the seashore...And by your offspring shall all the nations of the earth gain blessing for themselves..." (Genesis 22:17–18).

The connection between this verse and Mary's *Magnificat* is both vital and tender. God offers this blessing to Abraham at the time that Abraham has shown himself willing to sacrifice Isaac, his only son by Sarah, to God's will. For Abraham's sake, God spares Isaac. For our sake, God will not spare his own—and Mary's—Son. What God ultimately does not demand of his friend Abraham, he will demand of himself in order to decisively extend the promise and open his kingdom to all who believe in Jesus.

We don't have the sharp motivation of being convinced, as Paul, Peter, and the earliest Christians were, that Jesus will return in our lifetimes. We know, some two thousand years later, that God's plan is not our plan and God's time is not our time. We are still waiting. And therein lies our challenge today. Without the urgency, without the excitement, without, indeed, the fear of those first generations, we are in danger of letting both the joy and the responsibility of following Jesus fade from our lives. Knowing the tragedies of the past twenty centuries, the outrages committed against others, against God, sometimes falsely in God's name, we run the risk of being silenced by cynicism, sidelined by apathy, or paralyzed by horror. We live in an age when it is all too easy to go through the motions of hearing Mary and following Jesus without putting our hearts and minds and spirits into the work of God.

We must not grow weary or complacent! Remember when it was all new! Remember when God's promise and the fulfillment of that promise in Jesus of Nazareth were the only things worth living for! Remember every day to embrace the Holy Spirit! And imagine what it was like to be among those few Judeans who experienced in the words of one young, travel-worn girl from Nazareth the utter transformation of their world...and ours.

And Mary said, "According to the promise he made to our ancestors, to Abraham and his descendants forever."

Praying and Discussing the *Magnificat* Today

PRAYER

Mary, when you uttered your Spirit-given prayer, did you know how many of Abraham's descendants would depend upon the life of your Son? Did you know about the ones to come? Did you know about all those who would become spiritual descendants of Abraham through your Son? Did you know that he would open up his Father's promise to Gentiles, Egyptians, Greeks, Africans, Asians, people from every corner of the earth? Did you know that people would study his life and words for the rest of time? Did you know that his words—and yours—would be made new with every birth and death, baptism and confession, every celebration of the Holy Eucharist? Did you know how much he—and you—would suffer so as to set free the rest of the world for all time? Blessed Mother, how can I express my gratitude to you? Take me under your wing, teach me your humility, adopt me as your own child, and let me be joined in

this way to you and your Son, Jesus Christ: my Lord, my
Promise, my Fulfillment. Amen.

Questions

1. When you think of your biological ancestors, how far
   back do you go? When you consider your spiritual
   ancestors, how far back do you go? Do you believe
   yourself to be a descendant of Abraham? Do you feel
   that you are a child of God?

2. If you were among the Judeans who heard Mary and
   could—right now—speak to her, what would you say?